FOOD ON THE PLATE
WINE IN THE GLASS

Also by Max Lake

HUNTER, WINE
CLASSIC WINES OF AUSTRALIA
VINE & SCALPEL
THE FLAVOUR OF WINE
CABERNET
HUNTER WINEMAKERS
START TO TASTE: WINE (also in a Japanese edition)
START TO TASTE: FOOD
START TO TASTE: PEOPLE
SCENTS AND SENSUALITY (also in a Portuguese
   edition, and a Japanese one in progress)
SEVEN TONGUES (in preparation)

FOOD ON THE PLATE
WINE IN THE GLASS

According to the
workings and principles of
FLAVOUR

Max Lake

Dr Max Lake
PO Box 285
Manly NSW 2095
Australia

Tel: (02) 949 3156
Fax: (02) 977 0506

First published 1994

© Max Lake 1994

All rights reserved. No part of this publication may be reproduced, stored in a retrieval system, or transmitted in any form or by any means, electronic, mechanical, photocopying, recording, or otherwise, without the prior permission of the publisher.

Cover design and front cover photo by NB Design
Back cover photo and flavour brain sketch by the author
Editing, text design and typesetting by McMahon Publishing
Printed in Australia by Star Printery

National Library of Australia Cataloguing-in-Publication entry

Lake, Max.
  Food on the plate, wine in the glass.

  Bibliography.
  Includes index.
  ISBN 0 646 18147 5.

  1. Gastronomy. 2. Food. 3. Wine and wine making. 4. Taste.
  I. Title.

641.013

Life finally comes down to the six Fs. The prior drives have evolved from the calls of four of them, flight, fight, food and mate. The other two, flavour and fragrance, silhouette the enjoyment of food and the allure of love. Shortly, the table becomes one of the hallmarks of civilisation. Families are nourished, friendships flourish, gentle commerce is fostered, and amours all but consummated.

Contents

Foreword by Jancis Robinson — xi

Introduction & Allegro — 1

PART ONE
YOU AND FLAVOUR

1 Where We Are: The Renaissance — 9
  Food 9
  Wine 10
  People 11

2 How We Arrived: Evolution — 13
  The Idea of Flavour 13
  Taste Geography 14
  The Smell Brain 18
  The Chef/Sommelier's Brain 21
  Flavour Markers 22
  The Eye Gets the Upper Hand 23
  The Pleasure Factor 26

PART TWO
THE FLAVOURS OF FOOD AND WINE

3 Flavour Impact Compounds — 31
  Tastes 33
  Aromas 37

Sex, Again. The Sexual Pheromones 39
Hot and Cold 41
Wine 41
Echoes 43
Flavour Couplings 44

4 Food and Wine 45

Tradition in the West 45
Size and Balance — Big and Little 52
Manners 54
Cheeses 57
Jesus and the Sommelier 59
East Meets West 61

PART THREE
MATCHING FOOD AND WINE

5 Flavour Bridges 67

Cooking with Wine 67
The Chef/Sommelier's Brain in Action 68
Mother Sauces and a Master Sauce 70

CODA

6 Gastronomy: The Art of Flavour 75

Food Options 79

APPENDIX

Odour Classification 83
Pheromone Analogues in Food and Wine 84
Relative Sweetness 86
Reducing Sugar 86
Relative Sourness 87
Wine Acids and Palate Length 89
A Whimsical Depiction of the Brain of Flavour 91

Glossary	92
Biographical Notes	96
Acknowledgments	100
Recommended Reading	101
Index	103

Foreword

What fun it is to sit on the shoulder of one who achieves a unique treble. Max Lake is not only a wine authority who sees the kitchen as a natural extension of the cellar (a curiously unusual animal), but he is prepared, nay eager, to go into print with his thoughts on the complicated business of putting food and wine together.

He arrives at this particular minefield having already fought some valuable campaigns on neighbouring territory. When the world's food seers convene annually in the academic surroundings of St Anthony's College, Oxford, they anticipate the stimulus of this distinguished former surgeon and his radical conceptions of the senses of taste and smell.

And Max Lake's credentials as a winemaker aren't bad either. In 1963 he established a world famous winery from scratch, calling it, characteristically, Lake's Folly. When Australia's prolific, and highly opinionated, wine writer James Halliday has to describe his old Hunter Valley winemaking rival, this is how he does it:

> A legend in his own lifetime ... it is necessary to pay unstinting homage to the man who had the courage and foresight to show others it was possible for a dedicated amateur to plant a vineyard, erect his own winery and, without any outside technical assistance, proceed to make a great wine.

Max Lake's congenital enthusiasm is the final ingredient which makes the following pages inspirational rather than a turgid rule book. Which is just what a book about food and wine at the table should be.

Jancis Robinson
London, 1993

Introduction & Allegro

As this is my first affair
Would you kindly tell me what goes where.
> Ogden Nash, acc. to Hugo Dunn-Meynell

Why would anyone bother with yet another book on food and wine? Because here is a fresh approach to a problem which simply won't go away.

How often has delight mingled with surprise at the way the flavours of particular food and wine have come together? On the other hand, have you been disappointed and puzzled when they seemed to cancel out? Or worse, when after special planning and effort, you came up with something awful? If so, this book is for you. It is for all amateurs and professionals who buy or sell food or wine and for those who aim to set, and share, a great table.

More than 20 years ago, responding to an invitation from an influential Australian group, I struck a responsive chord. After dwelling on the classic table, the traditional white (wine) with white (food) and red (wine) with red (flesh), I touched on the concept of matching the intensity of *flavour* of the partners. It was an idea whose time was beginning, so that today this single principle has come to regulate many such unions. In a word, their SIZE is leading to the most appealing matches of the partners. The classic rules reign no longer, although they remain influential. Thus light wines sit with light food flavours and fuller bodied wines with gutsier tucker (G)*. During the past 20 years the quality of foods and wines has changed radically. Lifestyles have altered and a new perception and appreciation of flavour has flowered among those who look to the table for more than mere sustenance.

A brief review of the renaissance of flavour leads from how we have arrived at this point. The church steeples in the flavour landscape of food and wine are then described, followed by some of the methods of effecting flavour bridges between them. The work concludes with a new look at table manners, and some table fun.

There are many recipe books that deal completely or in part with the matching of food and wine. Some of the best are quoted in the text or mentioned in the reading list. *Food on the Plate, Wine in the Glass* does not cover the same ground, detailing but two recipes, and they are for sauces. Rather is it an opinionated work which seeks to reveal what a fondly remembered teacher used to call 'the story behind the story'. It assembles the principles of flavour perception in a fresh way, hopefully avoiding some of the misleading stuff from the past, even from those from whom better might have been expected. Because I have tried to lighten the stodge with some dried fruits and a few anecdotes, do not undervalue the import of the principles so garnished. My sympathy is extended to those who feel that knowledge destroys pleasure. For most, it is enhanced.

Some readers may hesitate upon realising that the

---

* In the text (G) denotes a Glossary entry.

evolution and neurology of taste and smell are described, albeit briefly. They are, however, the key to the best and simplest concept of how each of us perceives flavour. Communication is clear only with an understanding of the differences and dominants. Without it, we may not be talking about the same flavour. Deriving from good and useful science, this approach bids to extend your temptations and enjoyment. Yield to them, I beseech you, lest they leave you too soon.

Sixty years ago an Australian childhood, and an American mother, were not much of an introduction to the subject. Food was fresh but plain, wine avoided as too 'strong', or 'foreign'. On the rare night out, one encountered limited menus at a few pseudo-French restaurants, in Australia run mainly by Italians. Ethnic Chinese, Italian and Greek 'greasy spoons' were a big deal. The average Australian home had little cultural tradition to influence flavour preferences or cooking styles. With hindsight this may have been a virtue in that we had nothing much to unlearn. After the thirties, the buzz from travel and the waves of new immigrants rapidly filled the vacuum, to the point where Australian food has been in the vanguard of Pacific Rim cuisine, evolving a culinary mix that makes its many influential restaurants some of the most exciting in the world. During this recent crescendo, the wines of Australia have literally shocked the rest of the world by their fine quality and value.

Goodbye Culinary Cringe (1993) rejoiced in the present eminence of Australian food and wine on the international stage, no surprise to those who have laboured so long and hard to bring this about. My advice to the doubting traveller, especially those who think it better to travel than to arrive, is, simply, try it.

Elizabeth David, MFK Fisher, and Julia Child switched young chefs on to the pleasures of the table after World War II. My wife Joy, a country girl, with no pretensions to haute cuisine, became spectacularly creative after acquiring Ted Moloney's *Oh for a French Wife*, the small cookbook that fired our contemporaries in Oz. This coupled with my expanding experience of wine, a Hers-and-His bifid kitchen and a good wine cellar, and our natural competitiveness took flight. Confidence began to march with experience. We often did dinners course and course about, to the intrigued amusement of guests. It was get the wines right, or else. Or else, in the debriefing that invariably followed, trying to work out what had gone awry. We learnt the virtues of the classical food and wine marriages, and that transgression was not always folly. A transcendental match might be revealed. Perhaps it is the filter of time, but I seem to remember both the foods and wines were very good, and their unions comfortable and forgiving.

There have been extreme shifts in the simple flavours that were so fresh and definite at the family table of childhood. The efficiencies of production and distribution came to be driven by marketing demands for long 'shelf life'. The result was a calamity: food that looked good but had uniform or meagre flavour. The excitement of the comings and goings of seasonal foods all but disappeared. Happily now, smaller producers have initiated a pendulum swing back to freshness and clarity of flavour, so that not only do people realise what they have been missing, but the shared table has become more adventurous and enjoyable. Our palates and skills need to keep pace with the absolute improvements in the quality of available foods and wines.

People differ. This is often emphasised in the work,

because there is no absolute palate. You may not be out of step, just marching to a different drummer. Everyone has a range of 'odour blindness', and even your own tastes change with your bodily state.

It is not knowledge that destroys pleasure; rather are pretension and boredom the wreckers. Contrast and variety give it zest and are valuable teachers. A real understanding of the subject may come from an inspired professional, a gifted amateur, or a happy inspiration of your own. A single such flash can totally change your approach to the table. Exploring becomes exciting with fulfilled expectations. The more you experience, the better you become. *Don't get heavy about the subject, lest its essence, and its pleasure, elude you. A glass of quaffing red, crusty bread and a chunk of mature cheese is a nice escape from that common pitfall.*

Enjoy!

PART ONE

YOU AND FLAVOUR

1

Where We Are: The Renaissance

Food

The past 20 years have seen a celebration of the rebirth of flavour. The flavours and freshness of the fruit, vegetables, meat, fish and poultry available to the average city dweller have changed as radically as the population mix. So many forces, so many causes. Australia has a surfeit of natural goodies. A Saturday morning visit to public produce centres like the spectacular comet at Claremont in Perth, or those at Melbourne's Prahran, Adelaide or Flemington, or the Pyrmont fish market in Sydney, are mouthwatering excitements. Hypermarkets worldwide, often to be found in unexpected places, mirror the improvements, some of which are little short of sensational.

Fragrant roses are returning from an odourless limbo of half a century. Senile vegetables and fossil fruits are disappearing. Centres for further education in food and wine flourish. There are new varieties and species, and cultivation, harvesting, handling and distribution have all improved. Top chefs and shops have developed special relationships with talented producers. The loss of flavour quality from oxidation and poor refrigeration, and boring 'fast food', is less apparent now. One of the most obvious facets of the revolution in Western-style eating is the explosion in fast foods. The consumption of snails has declined. Japanese diet has taken a turn for the West. 'Takeaways' have become deservedly popular. The commercial demand for 'shelf life' was the cause of washed-out flavour, haunted by ghosts of childhood memories of definitive flavour delights ripe off the tree, or fresh out of the ground or water. Who remembers the taste of 'run-around chooks' that once delighted family Sunday tables? And they were big enough to satisfy a family. Or true lamb slow roasted in a big cast-iron fuel stove?

Wine

The new flavours of wine are in the vanguard of the renaissance. There was a polar change worldwide in the seventies. The fruit flavour of each variety has become clearer, the wines fresher and less likely to die suddenly in the bottle. Vineyard husbandry changed radically. The changes dwarf those of the twenties, when the introduction of destalking the bunches of grapes produced a remarkable softening and enhancement of flavour in the classic French wines. Now the vast improvement in winery practice has seen neglected fermentaries converted into spotless temples of hygiene. Mucky old barrels have gone to their reward as garden tubs or highway advertising signs. The use of high-grade stainless steel, inert to the aggressive chemical attack of wine, is now routine. Chateau Latour during the '67 vintage was unforgettable, the warm greeting of the *régisseur* almost neutralised by the rows of new, cold, inert steel fermenters. Offering a tray of tasting glasses, he asked if I could tell which wines were fermented in steel and which in the traditional large old wood vats. I couldn't find any differences. 'Neither can we,' he said.

Nowhere did the revolution bear more fruit than in Australia. The oldest land mass on the planet, it is a hard country that demands Australians become innovative, or fail. The proverbial 'cockie' (G), driving his battered ute or four-wheel drive around the back blocks, with a wire coat-hanger in the tool box, able to fix anything, is now legend.

Grange Hermitage has become an Australian icon. It appeared in the early fifties, fashioned from fruit flavour dense enough to make a junior port and matured in brand new small oak casks. These latter subsequently graduated to various Penfold 'bins', the St Henri's, the 707s, the 389s, whose balanced oak and fruit flavours led the wave of super quality commercial red wine in Australia. Incidentally, I trialled 12 barrels of different forest oaks with a uniform wine of the same vintage in the sixties to determine which flavour married best with the wine I was developing. That was years before the Californian efforts of everybody's buddy, Robert Mondavi, bless him.

People

Recognition of the effects of diet and activity on health has been slow. There has been a sea change in the foods eaten in pursuit of a 'healthy' diet. People now seek freshness and balance. Even so, it is still difficult to escape troglodytes who continue to serve sequences of saturated fat foods at grand banquets or in the pressurised cabins of aircraft five miles high.

Clearly the classical marriages of food and wine, which worked well, have become less relevant as lifestyle and the flavour spectrum have changed. Mixes of

Eastern, Western and Mediterranean cuisines continue with bewildering speed.

So food and wine flavour have changed, as has lifestyle. What of the perception of flavour, a major preoccupation of the author over the past half century?

2

How We Arrived: Evolution

The Idea of Flavour

Flavour is a seamless fabric fashioned from experience.

In ordinary everyday activity we don't go around actually thinking about, much less analysing, bodily function. Unless we stop to think, or our attention is actively directed, we don't single out sensations or, for that matter, single ingredients of food or drink. However, there is an instant and instinctive like/dislike reaction in those who are ready to perceive a flavour or fragrance. It is a quantitative assessment, in that, for example, we like it a lot, or not much. Children are forthright in their 'yum' and 'yuk'. Once one starts to reflect, there are layers and depths in the response.

The thinking brain has come up with the idea of flavour by combining the messages of smell, taste, and the other sensations. *Every flavour begins with taste and smell.* We are now going to consider these components, always remembering that the end result is a totality to which we will react positively or negatively, if we are paying attention.

As far as I am aware, this is the first grouping of the sensory sequences which create a perception of flavour that is structured on the evolution of the initial relay stations of these senses in the central nervous system (see Figure 2, 'A Whimsical Depiction of the Brain of Flavour', on page 91). Again, is it presumptuous to wonder if neurologists and flavourists have ever sat at a table together and attempted the precise cross-fertilisation I have attempted here? I hope I'm not reinventing the wheel. I have chosen this synthesis as the best way to avoid the unbelievable confusion that reigns in some widely read tomes that deal with taste and flavour, and in the teaching of some respected schools which ought to know and teach better.

Taste Geography

'A taste of honey.' 'Vanilla flavour.' We use the *words* taste and flavour interchangeably, but to sharpen your perception of wine and food, it must be remembered that you actually go about the acts of tasting with the mouth, and smelling with the nose. There are at least ten tastes and perhaps 20 aroma families. When these combine in the brain, the idea of flavour is born. If the nose is blocked, for example with a cold, the odour input stops, unless a little of it gets up the back of the nose from something in the mouth. We then say the food or drink 'has no taste', although salty or sweet things, for example, are still *tasted* in the mouth. Just realise how we shift the word 'taste' around in everyday use.

Before we begin to examine how this fresh idea of flavour developed, a few words might be in order on how we happened on a suitable first model. Seeking a model of the early organisation of flavour and fragrance signals in living organisms, the earthworm seemed a logical choice, for the following reasons. In its elementary simplicity, it has a simple cylindrical body, a tubed gut that goes from one end to the other, and a primitive nervous system that encircles the mouth end forming the semblance of a kind of brain. The gut continues in a virtual straight line down to the other, 'bottom', end.

In the course of checking just what might be derived from their sapid surroundings, some riveting facts about the sex life of the not so humble earthworms came to light during the research. These could well form a starting point for anyone who feels inclined to do for sex what I am attempting to do for flavour and fragrance. For example, in the words of Hy Freedman, from his book about a 3 billion-year-old urge, 'Since worms spend most of their lives underground in pitch blackness, even they might have problems sorting each other out.' It will come as no surprise that this early animal form is a complete hermaphrodite, with both male and female bits. A cute solution, short circuiting the guy/doll problem of identical and pheromone-free body forms in the darkness. But we tarry too long.

We do have full use of a *taste brain*, inherited from lowly forms of life after tens of millions of years, that is, the chemical sensations perceived by a worm. They register as sweet, sour, salty and bitter from the tip, sides and back of the tongue, respectively. There is a recently recognised fifth taste, from the depths of a soup stock, called umami, defined by Professor Kikunae Ikeda around 1909 as 'a delicious or savoury quality'. These five primary tastes first pass to the brain stem, to the solitary nucleus and its tract, adjacent to which the primary life support systems, like heart rate, vomiting (for speedy rejection of taste threats, for example) and breathing, also reside (see Figure 2, 'A Whimsical Depiction of the Brain of Flavour', on page 91).

The worm-like taste brain has other motor, reflex, responses. None are more striking than the facial expressions of the new baby, as it responds to sweet or sour tastes, for example. There is not the slightest doubt of the infant's feelings. The wonder is that it arrives complete with memory and response to these and other tastes, programmed during a vast stretch of evolutionary experience.

What do earthworms taste? Easier to say what they don't smell, lacking the brain and sensors for whatever airborne aromas might be around. They do have a chemical sense, though, sensing molecules by contact. By analogy it seems reasonable to assume that they probably do have an ability to get some sort of a buzz out of saltiness, acids in the soil, those molecules we will later call sweet, and the bitterness of plant alkaloids that may well be quite nasty, even life threatening. And what of umami, the brothy taste? Well, certainly if they are Japanese worms, or receptive Western sorts.

So at the beginning of the flavour cascade we can imagine the mapping of an earthworm's taste brain. During the earlier stages of evolution it may have developed to ensure the integrity and function of the cell, in the following manner:

SOUR ($H+$)	Controls ionic balance within the narrow zone essential for life.
SALT ($Na+$)	Stabilises the composition of the body's internal sea.
UMAMI (MSG)	Assists the building of cell protein.
SWEET	For the energy exchange of cell activity.
BITTER	Warns of the toxic threats to cell integrity.

This starts to explain why the primary tastes are so potent, and thus their relevance in cooking.

There is a second taste system, which is simply part of the body's perception of sensation generally, except that the information comes from the start of the alimentary tract, that is, the mouth and its neighbourhood. Pain elsewhere becomes the pungency of chilli or mustard in the mouth. Hot and cold likewise. The body sensors that determine the various kinds of touch, position and tension, for example of a limb, combine in the mouth to define the texture and mouth-feel of different foods and liquids. We can tell the difference between oil, water, honey and cream; between sand, nuts or gritty granules; and between lettuce and cooked cabbage. When the protective mucus cover of the tongue and cheeks is coagulated, for example by wine tannin, we speak of astringency.

So to summarise, taste has two quintets. The first, comprising the sensations of sour, salty, sweet, bitter and umami, registers in the worm's taste brain. The trigeminal (G) five are pain/pungent, hot/cold, texture/crunch, mouth-feel, and astringent. There are other debated tastes, like metallic. They all make it to the thalamus (G) and ultimately relay to the most recently evolved higher brain centres in the postcentral gyrus (G). Smell, on the other hand, gets straight to the smell brain without a thalamic relay.

Palate length (see Figure 1, 'Wine Acids and Palate Length', on page 89) refers to the time factor in assessing a taste mix. The Riedel Glass Company conduct tastings which show how the perception of the flavour of a wine varies with the shape of the glass. The classic tasting glass with rim narrower than the waist (to concentrate the bouquet) contrasts with the large glass with wide rim (the 'Burgundy glass'). A sip of wine is presented in a different time sequence and to a different area of the mouth in each case. The big glass favours the structure of a Pinot wine. Try it.

In *Wine with Food* (1975), Cyril and Elizabeth Ray recalled how Bertrand Russell, then 17, was left alone with the 80-year-old Prime Minister Gladstone, awaiting 'the pearls of political wisdom that might fall from those awesome lips'. There was a silence that the boy feared to break, and then the PM exclaimed, 'This is a very good port they have given me, but why have they given it to me in a claret glass?' Nearly 70 years later, when he was 85 years old, Russell wrote, 'I did not know the answer, and wished the earth would swallow me up. Since then I have never again felt the full agony of terror.'

Palate length can be demonstrated by comparing some wine acids in the concentrations they might naturally occur. The tasting of each acid must be separated by vigorous rinsing of the mouth with distilled water, to clear the palate for the next test. The tasting must be done in sequence, with malic first, tartaric next, and acetic last. The hardness of the latter really lasts; that is, it has an *aftertaste*. Even longer is the 'tannin' component, or tannic and wood acids, as they were sometimes called by traditional winemakers. Taste has many unique features. For one, it tends to less fatigue with repetition, unlike smell.

The Smell Brain

While the chemical *contact* sense we have come to know as taste guided the worm's activities, other life forms, on the earth and in the water, were developing the ability to sense *distant* particles, delivered by either air or water. Smell became the first sense to pick up remote messages, some of which were warnings of potential threats, others indicators of positive benefit like food or sex. A storage facility was elaborated along with this talent, and the remembering, thinking, discriminating and creative brain that we now recognise as the cerebral cortex was on its way. Some of the great neurologist philosophers of the earlier part of the twentieth century, William Le Gros Clark and Frederick Wood Jones in particular, considered that the cortex, newest development of the human brain, evolved from the rudimentary olfactory functional demands. In short, *we are, because we smell.*

The smell brain was then considered to encompass the hypothalamic automotive control system of all body function, including endocrine glands. As the various connections of the hypothalamus have become better understood, they have come to be regarded as a working unity, the limbic system. This is now understood to influence the reciprocating balance and tuning of the more recently evolved cortex. It is a matter of some regret that the concept of a smell brain has fallen into disuse. It is still possible to discuss fairly clear anatomical and functional divisions of the relays and results. We shall proceed to examine these, and how they may affect our food and wine, and the matching and enjoyment thereof.

Continuing research in this field confirms what certain Western individuals and many Eastern faiths have long been aware of: the unity of human mind/emotion and physical function, which is merely mentioned here to encourage the idea that there is more than just the pleasures of the table involved in our subject.

There have been three golden ages of the smell brain, and each continues to influence our flavour and fragrance responses. The first reached its peak in the cuddly koala (or hedgehog if you are so inclined), half of whose brain is occupied with olfaction. Up an evolutionary gum tree, the smell brain was never to be as big, relatively, again. The flavour and fragrance input to the human brain has fallen to less than a fifth of all the incoming messages.

An *accessory, sexual, smell brain* reached its golden age in reptiles and amphibians like crocodiles, who, incidentally, are reliably reported to have a preference for female humans. (Beef and pork of female origin has a finer flavour than its male counterpart.) Reptiles have a fully developed sexual odour and taste system, whose receiver is situated between the eyes, just below the surface. It is called the vomeronasal (from the bones that encompass it) organ of Dr Jacobson. If you want to know approximately where the outlet of the human remnant is, stick the tongue on your hard palate just above the central incisor teeth. Its vestige lies deep in the brain itself. A complete and fascinating anatomical replay of all these phases of the evolution of smell and taste is seen during the early development of the human embryo (G).

Those fortunate enough to possess a working vestige of the accessory smell brain will pick up the five sexual pheromones (G) (see Table 1, 'Odour Classification', on page 83). Those which impact on food and wine flavour will be discussed later (see 'Sex, Again. The Sexual Pheromones' on page 39). Researching the subject, it has been amazing to learn that these emotive molecules were likely influences on the sexual activity of cells in hot swamps 400 million years ago.

Debate continues about the persistence of sexual smell brain function in humans. The doubters may well be odour blind. Not really a form of odour blindness, others subconsciously refuse to react to certain odours after they register, although experimental brain scans clearly show this has taken place At the same time, they claim not to smell anything, inhibition by any other name. Some are threatened by observing the odour drive of our nearest animal relations. Denial is not going to make it go away. This subject is developed as a major theme of *Fragrances of Love*, as yet unpublished.

*The Chef/Sommelier's Brain**

The third olfactory component of the modern brain also has a golden age. It is now. The huge 'new' (from the evolutionary point of view) cerebral hemispheres house the computer and memory bank where all the inputs of smell and taste are finetuned and creatively developed.

From the functional viewpoint many people can't pick more than three components of an odour, and very few more than five. But rest assured everyone can improve with training, even many of those who have 'odour blindness'. Some specially gifted people are said to be able to discriminate a considerable number of the 10,000 single odours thought to exist.

What better name for it than the 'chef/sommelier's brain'? Unless it is called the 'wine taster's brain'. Although a bloodhound might have 40 times as efficient a smell brain (advanced koala model), it might, on occasion, happily swap with us.

Aromas easily fall into about 20 family groups, from which derive all the natural and synthetic odours known. One of the clearest classifications is from Kurt Bauer, Dorothea Garbe, and Horst Surburg (modified) (see Table 1, 'Odour Classification', on page 83).

---

* sommelier: a highly qualified wine steward (Fr.)

How often have you failed to perceive a flavour or fragrance that was obvious to someone nearby? Or failed to convince your partner that a certain character was present? There are dozens of such gaps of 'blindness' and everyone has some of them. Don't let it obtrude on your enjoyment. It is, however, just as well to know that you don't perceive bitter or burnt, for example, as easily as others. It seems to be one of Nature's droller ripostes that one who can't smell burnt toast takes up residence with a 'significant other' who can. Which may explain François Rabelais' remark:

> Everyone to their own taste, as the woman said kissing her cow.

Flavour Markers

The disproportionate impacts of some flavours have come to be danger warnings, markers of nutritional essentials, improvers of body function, or sexual invitations. Nature has given such flavours an extra impact as an important survival value. We are programmed to perceive these in amounts that are so minute it is a marvel they can be sensed at all. Why else would the 'green' aroma of the pyrazine MIP (G) be so extraordinarily potent that one drop in an Olympic swimming pool is noticeable? It is *the* 'green' flavour, that of cut green grass or capsicum/bell pepper, the pyrazine MIP, or IMP. Ron Buttery proposes it as a marker for the presence of life supporting vitamin C, which humans are alone among animals in their inability to synthesise. Its flavour impact in either food or wine may be so assertive as to disturb a respectable match.

Thiamin (vitamin B1) has much the same 'marker'

intensity and is essential for the integrity of nerves. The special power of MSG, *the* umami taste, suggests it may be a marker for essential protein acids. Bitterness is certainly a warning of toxic alkaloids in plants. We tend to get a special pleasure (endorphin [G] release) from the flavours of foods that foster nutrition or reproduction.

From simple cells in the muck of a hot swamp, via an evolutionary line that includes worms, reptiles, koalas, and apes, there has been a gradual progress to the extraordinary finetuning of the nose of a super smeller, whether it adorn the face of a mother, a chef, a sommelier, a winemaker or a perfumer. Even though some obviously start well ahead of the mob, we can all improve by training.

The Eye Gets the Upper Hand

Seeing is deceiving. It's eating that's believing.
James Thurber

It was but a blink of evolutionary time after animals got up from four legs to two, when sight began to dominate smell. However, olfaction is still quite capable of briefly regaining its primacy under special circumstances, for example, when we suddenly perceive the smell of something burning.

Food and wine at the table may stand or fall on the visual message. The two-legged inspectors of the *Guide Michelin* award the second star for presentation. We are inclined to label something by appearance, rather than taste. Flavour perception is 'confirmed' by seeing, and even hearing, food or drink. Professional wine judges allocate about 15% of the marks to the appearance of the wine. Experience teaches that depth of colour and hue give some idea of the growing season of the fruit, the crop level, and the winery technique. Michael Broadbent's pocket book on wine tasting has the colours down pat.

Experiments with coloured sweetened water have been known to humble even wine judges. Try someone with this food colour test. Set up two glasses of plain water containing identical amounts of sugar and a food acid at about their strengths in fruit juice. Tint them with food colours, one red and the other green (even better with light red and orange colours). An innocent palate will often find the made-up flavours different, and if pressed may suggest a range of berry and citrus fruits. If there is a glass of the real stuff alongside each for comparison, you will be astonished at the results. This is the equivalent of wine 'label drinking', of which, may I hasten to add, we are all capable. Don't get too uppity! A deep turquoise sauce (flour and water) was specifically coloured by Tony Bohdan of the Chevron without prior warning, as a test of our honesty, in the innocent halcyon days of long ago. This was served with a chunk of unseasoned stark white boiled fish. It was difficult to stomach, and was universally panned. (Has anyone ever enjoyed a bright blue sauce?) Having passed that test, members of the Chevron Friday table graduated to the good stuff.

Twenty years ago, the power of visual input was amply demonstrated on a moonlit night on a bush road after a dinner at Chateau Tahbilk. Our driver stopped the car, went to the boot and produced a bottle and poured wine into some white enamel tin mugs. What did I think of it? I couldn't tell, in truth could scarcely get any nose either. It happened to be a Chateau Margaux of a great year, but only when told so did I start to make it fit my conception of the wine. Perhaps this says more about my palate than the dominance of visual input, or, in this instance, confusing lack of it.

Before passing on to more practical considerations, there is an analogy of 'label drinking' that I call 'head food'. Can it be possible to taste in your mind? If you are one of those people who has difficulty in dropping off to sleep reading a good food or wine book, to the extent that you have to go and check the fridge, you will understand the question, and the concept.

Paul and Penny Levy had arrived at the home of Julia Child in the hills above Grasse. In his words:

> For lunch we had home-made *foie gras* served with toast fingers and 'Ivan's Aperitif'. One measure dry white French vermouth, such as dry Martini or Noilly Prat; one measure sweet white vermouth or white Lillet or white Dubonnet; one tablespoon gin (which gives an unctuous quality to the cocktail and is therefore an essential ingredient) and a 6 cm strip of fresh zest of orange. Pour the vermouths over several ice cubes in a clear long stemmed wine glass. Float the gin on the surface, but do not stir. Squeeze the zest over the glass, then rub it around the rim and pop it into the drink.

After reading that, who could contain themselves in the middle of the night? I got out of bed and proceeded with the recipe. Except, as an inveterate fiddler, I used exquisitely ripe tangerines (which grow well at Lake's Folly) instead of the orange. And then, absolutely delighted with the results, I phoned Paul (it was okay, daytime in London) to share the moment.

Everyone eats with their eyes first.

The Pleasure Factor

Even if you are one of those Puritans who merely 'eats to live', you would have to be aware that some things 'taste good'. Like the rest of humankind, you are experiencing the effects of a release of happy hormones from the smell brain and related structures that follows on eating the things that are 'good' for us. (We are talking about people in normal health here. The drive for excessive sugar or salt, for example, may be a sign of disease). This is simply the consequence of millions of years of evolution, and the greatest performers in the kitchen instinctively follow this program. Consider the depth of flavour enhancement from the use of good stocks, the balance of acids and sweetness, or the delights of getting a food/wine match spot on. These, and other examples of harmony, further increase enjoyment. Some such events may see the shared table afloat in a flood of endorphins (G). Conversely, it is a sad day when one's efforts are tolerated, or worse, as the food and wine battle it out.

Never ignore that cardinal principle of flavour and fragrance, namely that we most enjoy them when they are only just perceived. LESS IS MORE. Always! There is an inevitable path from delight to disgust, discussed at some length in *Scents and Sensuality*. Just ponder the startling example of putrid seafoods, like blachan, dried extract of rotten little prawns, minuscule amounts of which give so much of the charm to South-East Asian cuisine; or the fish sauces of the Mediterranean of ancient times.

The mention of Eastern cooking calls to mind another source of table pleasure, the pungency of chilli, mustard, pepper and the like. Why do many people seek out this heat, the incandescence of which may actually put the palate out of action, and certainly limits the beverage matches to yoghurt drinks, beer, cider, or wind-assisted wines (only joking!) of varieties like the Traminer grape? According to one hypothesis, it is the pain. It releases endorphins (G). Well, it is an explanation.

PART TWO

THE FLAVOURS OF FOOD AND WINE

3

Flavour Impact Compounds

Have you ever been out in the country and, coming over the top of a rise, paused to take in the vista of the valley below? A stream runs beside the road winding through a small collection of cottages. A church steeple rises high among them to puncture the tranquillity. That church steeple symbolises a *flavour impact compound* (FIC), which stands out from the balanced elements of flavour in the general landscape of our food and drink. If FICs clash, the union is a mess, remembered only for the futility of the preparation. Occasionally they cancel out, leaving behind a ghostly puzzle. If they achieve a degree of equality, harmony prevails: a happy meal. If they actually complement each other, there are the foundations of a great occasion at the table.

You may have found the preceding discussion of the evolution of taste dry bones compared to tasting at a table, but some understanding of it will put you a country mile ahead in your encounters with flavour. The best matches of food with wine occur if you understand the concept of FICs, now to be discussed in a sequence suggested by 'The Idea of Flavour' (see page 13).

Some flavour impact compounds boost flavour when present in appropriate amounts in food. Added MSG could be the twentieth century prototype of flavour power. Ordinary salt has filled that role since the dawn of history. Unknown in wine, MSG is added to a vast range of manufactured foods worldwide. It is naturally present in tasty foods. All stocks, be they meat, fish or vegetable, get a flavour lift from glutamates (G) and similar compounds.

Here are some of Charles Dickens' thoughts on the matter:

> 'It's a stew of tripe,' said the landlord, smacking his lips, 'and cow-heel,' smacking them again, 'and bacon,' smacking them once more, 'and steak,' smacking them for the fourth time, 'and peas, cauliflowers, new potatoes, and sparrow-grass, all working up together in one delicious gravy.'
>
> *The Old Curiosity Shop*

> 'There is no such passion in human nature, as the passion for gravy among commercial gentlemen. It's nothing to say a joint won't yield - a whole animal wouldn't yield - the amount of gravy they expect each day at dinner and what I have undergone in consequence,' cried Mrs Todgers, raising her eyes and shaking her head, 'no-one would believe!'
>
> *Martin Chuzzlewit*

Tomato concentrates, some cheeses, particularly aged parmesan, and some mushrooms are especially potent sources of MSG. Umami has been described as the taste of MSG, which may also, to some people, be perceived as 'metallic'.

Balancing FICs in wine and food can become a minefield. A tiny amount of a new synthetic, sotolon, has been shown to be a FIC capable of simulating much of the charm of botrytised, 'sticky' wines. However, synergism (G) with similar molecules in foods can give a curry note! That is why one must continually taste and be ready to modify as often as necessary. Some FICs work at stunningly low levels. The delectable floral note of some teas, like jasmine, comes from amounts as little as half a part per billion of the brewed tea. It is 400 times stronger than its 'twin' isomer (G), methyl jasmonate.

Tastes

Sweet

Sweet is the fastest gun in the west, the quickest taste to be perceived in isolation. Sweetness is the energy marker. It adds to mouth-feel. It has an emotional bonus, the ability to evoke warm and pleasant feelings. It shuts down appetite.* Cold lessens its perception. Matching takes some experience because the amount present is so easily masked, for example by acid. Have you ever tried 'sweetening' lemon or lime juice?

Desserts are among the easier food and wine matches. Their natural partner is a 'sticky' wine. Even here relative 'sizes' of food and wine are important, of which more in 'Size and Balance — Big and Little' on page 52. The relative sweetness of various sugars and sweeteners is listed in Table 3 on page 86.

It is not widely realised that when tasting a wine which is perceptibly sweet (not quite 'dry' in ordinary terms), the bouquet is lifted compared to an otherwise identical wine. Sweetness also adds a certain fullness to the body of flavour. Fruit flavour itself may suggest sugar sweetness, but such wines can test virtually nil for reducing sugar. A lingering aftertaste of sweetness is a clear indication of actual residual sugar (see Table 4, 'Reducing Sugar', on page 86). The time it persists is directly related to the amount present. That is why

---

* Paradoxically, it can rekindle it in some individuals.

Serena Sutcliff has been seen to click her stopwatch many seconds after tasting a wine.

Bitterness masks sweetness. 'Dry' vermouth is 4% sugar! Wines high in alcohol taste sweeter and match well with slightly sweet food, for example, a stew with a fried onion base or lots of carrots, or an onion-finished chicken (sauce soubise, for example). Added sugar is one of the most widely used modern commercial flavour boosters. A substantial part of South-East Asian cuisine relies on it.

Sour

Sourness registers in 4–8 seconds, depending on the sort of acid, how much there is of it, and what else comes with it. Vinegar (acetic) acid is picked up at about 0.012%, while mineral hydrochloric acid hits at 0.008%. Some foods have a typically high single acid, for example rhubarb (oxalic) and grapes (tartaric). (See Table 5, 'Relative Sourness', on page 87.)

The sour taste of many foods and drinks may well give a flavour impact that demands a bridge on particular occasions in the kitchen and at the table. The acidity of wines tends to be less of a problem than that of foods when matching the two. Food acids generally need to be balanced with some sleight of hand in the kitchen before the wine makes its appearance. Otherwise at the table the wine becomes rather pallid. Wine acids are a special study in themselves, lifting middle palate and contributing to the impression of palate length (see Figure 1, 'Wine Acids and Palate Length', on page 89). Wine buffs will know that the secondary fermentation of malic acid in wine produces the softer tasting lactic acid, evident in red wine and many whites. Lime juice is among the most acid of foods and Mocha coffee perhaps the most acid of all coffees. The acid lift in its middle palate is quite characteristic.

In principle, it should be a simple matter to balance the tartness of a wine with an equivalent acid addition to the food, or to choose a lively wine to match the salad dressing. In practice, fortune flavours the brave.

The experienced cook adjusts acidity by adding where necessary (lemon or other fruit juices, vinegar), altering its perception (oil or sugar) or even subtracting (milk, starches). The winemaker avoids a flat mawky palate by picking at the correct balance of sugar and acid in the fruit on the vine, or adjusting it afterwards.

Sourdough breads attract the most creative breadmakers, because their efforts are so much appreciated for the 'natural' exciting lift of flavour. Lionel Poilane, Parisian master baker, thinks sour is the most important taste.

Salt

Salt is unquestionably the most common flavour booster. Perception of the sodium ion is the mirror of our internal ocean, a reminder of the composition of the sea at the period when life forms quit it. Tracks made by animals in the pursuit of salt were later used as trade routes and are among the earliest roads in all history.

In normal health, the body strives to maintain equilibrium in the internal sea, but the level of palate preference can be easily reset. Thirty years ago it was observed that a tribe of wild Japanese monkeys used to wash soil from their food with fresh water. Following the experiment of a young female, they subsequently used sea water in preference to fresh.

As a FIC, excessive salt is most simply dealt with by accompaniments like salt-free potatoes or rice. Salty wines are uncommon. They are technically faulty.

Pain/Pungent

> There is a particular man who delights in having as few needs as possible. He carries with him a little flour, a pinch of salt and chillies tied in his napkin.
>
> Mahatma Gandhi

Pungent FICs, of which the chilli burn has to be the hallmark, are relatively slow to register. Who can forget the stealth with which it creeps up, and wham! In handling them raw, take care of eyes and those other delicate bits. The pungency of chilli, wasabe, mustard and so on is the beginning of pain. (As a closet neurologist, I wonder why such an important signal starts in free nerve endings. There should have been a better way.) Chilli usually deserves its reputation as a wrecker of flavour matches. The burn certainly knocks mouth taste about, for a while. The aromas with which such food is associated, either Eastern or Western in origin, are often impenetrable by good wine. Fruity wines are about as close a match as one can get. Have you ever tried dry cider with a curry? They seem made for each other.

Astringency

Astringency has a considerable impact on the flavour mixes of wine and food. Fats and oils immediately soften the harshness of wine tannins. Mixing and matching wines with cheeses is an art of its own. Oz Clarke and Robert Joseph have made special studies of the problem of accentuated tannin notes in wines served in high altitude, pressurised cabins. Wine may become a ghostly skeleton except for its finish. It is regrettable how this is still ignored by otherwise expert wine selection panels of certain major airlines. Heaven knows their food, too, could often use some help.

Aromas

MIP or IMP is shorthand for a particular member of the pyrazine family of compounds (G). It is a major part of the aroma of fresh cut green grass, bell peppers, capsicum, green olives, some young wines of Cabernet Sauvignon and Sauvignon (Fumé) Blanc grapes and occasionally other varietal white wines. It may be apparent in beans, spinach, gooseberries, Kiwi fruit, Hungarian goulash and so on. Although most people like a moderate amount of it, there are some who can't handle it at any level, the dreaded *'pipi de chat'*. Judging wine recently with Heidi Peterson, I was reminded that this is a more elegant way of saying *cat's piss*.

One drop of MIP is said to be perceptible in a 50-metre pool. It is often *the* problem FIC. Green, the simple colour green, is emotionally felt to be 'good', especially in fresh vegetables, or the slightest hint of green in a limpid white wine. The pyrazine (G) family are at the heart of our favourite green and brown flavours.

As the energy of the sun and light elaborates green flavours, so does fire define many brown flavours. Dr Maillard discovered the flavours of the reaction named for him by heating amino acids with a sugar.

Kitchen-wise children of my era soon learnt that if the heating of sugar is arrested before it becomes charcoal, various shades of attractive caramel result. (The result of heating a tin of condensed sweetened milk for an hour in boiling water was a special revelation and became a great treat to be shared by the teaspoonful.) Apart from a special series of caramel flavours, their colour contributes to the visual appeal of whatever they are legally added to. The dozens of Maillard brown flavours are chemical siblings of the green IMP/MIP. Many have a powerful impact. Among them are the roasts and toasts, tea, coffee, chocolate, beer, whisky, and part of the oak flavour in wine. A note of caution. A browned unfortified 'white' table wine is oxidised and spoiled, but certain brown fortified-with-alcohol wines (e.g. madeira or Muscat) are naturally built that way.

Insects continue to share our enthusiasm for pyrazines, with trail pheromones that smell of roast beef, cocoa, coffee, and roasted nuts. Was he also a chef who wrote, 'Go thee to the ant, thou sluggard. Consider her ways and be wise.'? The staves of oak barrels are fashioned by toasting and bending them over a charcoal brazier. When the toasty oak melds with maturing red or white wine, such wines may benefit vastly from the liaison. Don't neglect vegetables at the 'barbie'; browning them often forms an excellent bridge to wine.

Floral, fruity and spicy FICs may be conveniently discussed here. All ripe fruit and flower fragrances are vital signals of plants' reproductive cycles. Sometimes an invitation to fertilisation, other times they ensure that fruit is eaten and seeds disseminated. The Middle Eastern use of rosewater encourages some exotic food and wine mixes. Ouzo, arrack, pernod (anise) are powerful drinks to reckon with. The aromas of spices like pepper, cloves, cinnamon and fennel and herbs like mint, basil and liquorice may be encountered in many wines. They are FICs and need to be recognised to be tamed and integrated. They demand similar flavours in food, or vice versa, where possible. A fuller list is given later (see Table 1, 'Odour Classification', on page 83). The wine of Traminer (Gewurtz='spice'-traminer) and cousins like Muscat may evoke a mix of carnation flowers and cloves, sit well beside the most aromatic dish, and are naturals for 'difficult' oriental and South-East Asian meals.

Sex, Again. The Sexual Pheromones

Pheromone (G) is a recent coinage from the Greek for 'transfer of excitement'. Pheromones excite a response in members of the same species by the perception of air- or water-borne molecules (olfaction by any other name). The first pheromone to be discovered had a sexual function, but the term has a far wider application now. Hormones are also chemical messengers. The difference is that they shuttle around *inside* the body. The crossovers between pheromones, hormones, nerve transmitters (G) and emotion have been explored in *Sex and the Single Cell* (unpublished).

A wide range of food and wine flavours are powered by pheromonal FICs. The most complex is androstenone (G), the male musk, which may suggest honey, cedar or sandalwood to those who are able to perceive it. Of more than 20 analogues, 5-alpha- may closely resemble the bouquet of certain fine mature Cabernet Sauvignon red wines. Roast beef with a truffled madeira glaze reeks of it. Some soft cheeses and a few champagnes have more than a hint of the feminine IVA (G).

> An escaper from a World War Two prison camp in Malaya lived for years on rice and minuscule amounts of blachan[*] supplied by friendly natives. He claimed his survival was in no small measure due to the flavour.
>
> From *Scents and Sensuality*, 1991

Two of the most potent flavour boosters are ancient: the classic TMA (G) of marine compost (fish, oyster,

---

[*] Made from sun-dried rotting prawns. Stinks of TMA (G), which in careful additions adds to the flavour of much South-East Asian food.

prawn and anchovy sauces and pastes) and the musk of early China and India. You would be amazed at the improvement in flavour of many modern canned foods and drinks from the addition of minuscule amounts of musk or the more complex of its synthetic equivalents. There is a table of food flavours that suggests the sexual pheromones on page 84.

The truffle/androstenone/Cabernet relationship may seem a bit far-fetched to some readers. Ponder the following observation from Timothy Pak Poy, of Claude's (a top Sydney restaurant), who had been doing a very slow reduction of a Cabernet wine over several hours for a special sauce. A fellow chef walked into the kitchen, now redolent of the pot fragrance, and immediately asked to know where such marvellous fresh truffles were to be obtained in Sydney. The cassis (black currant) note of an oak-matured Cabernet translates, with age or the heat of a slow reduction, to cedar and sandalwood oils, and sometimes to truffles and androstenone. I have elsewhere described the 'turned-on' dining group of ladies and gentlemen, under the sway of a roast sirloin served with the beef juice reduction finished with truffles and madeira to make the glaze. Madeira and truffles synergise with the potent umami boost of a beef reduction. Take a Cabernet wine with it, and Bob's (or Roberta's) your uncle (or aunt?). Score at least one more failure of the rhythm method of population control.

Androstenone and TMA are challenging FICs. When on the border of being barely perceptible (just above threshold), they are widely appreciated. Stronger than this in foods and the match with wine is difficult, and they become turn-offs in themselves. 'Less is more' remains the ultimate declaration of style. 'Less may be better' should be on every kitchen wall.

Hot and Cold

The temperature of wine or food merits special mention because of the often unexpected flavour impact. If too cold the flavour is washed out. Masking excessive sweetness or off-flavours in chilled wines is a well known vendor's trick. Moreover restaurateurs are not going to spend all that money on expensive ice buckets and not have them used. No siree! A hot room or a summer's day may indicate five minutes chilling of a wine, but watch it. A red wine can be left naked except for its tannin.

The flavours of fat emulsions at different temperatures can be remarkably different. Fat is a storage medium for some flavours and they can be lost or masked (G) in very hot food. Just think of the differences between the flavours of hot and cold milk coffee, or made-up meat dishes; a terrine or meat loaf is always more toothsome eaten cold, next day. A new perspective on wine temperature and food matching is discussed in 'East Meets West' on page 61.

Wine

It may be helpful to have a short list of the usual aromas that may be encountered in table wines, as so many of them make a powerful impact (see table on next page).

	Aroma of the grape	**Bouquet of the wine**
White grapes		
Muscat	typical, intense	rose, geranium, spicy
Traminer	carnation, clove	spicy
Riesling	tropical fruit, guava, lychee and so on	continues
Semillon	ripe green-skinned small fruits*, e.g. plum; also capsicum	fresh straw, fruity, honey
Sauvignon Blanc	capsicum, bell pepper	spicy, intense
Chardonnay	citrus peel, grapefruit, lime; fig, melon, yeast	peach, apricot, quince, hazelnut, butter, toast, cinnamon, honey
Red grapes		
Cabernet Sauvignon**	blackcurrant, bell pepper, mint, black cherry	cedar oil, cigar box, liquorice, small berries & flowers, butter, leather, truffles
Pinot Noir	ripe fruit	strawberry, beetroot, little flowers, plum (red)
Gamay	raspberry	persists
Shiraz, Hermitage	blackberry	black pepper, musky
Oak (source)	can be toasty, or not	
Limousin	vanilla, chocolate	
Nevers	resiny, lemon	
Memmel	orange peel	
Missouri	floral, jam	

Yeast Many yeasts have other characters than just 'yeasty'. 'Fresh bread', 'tropical fruit', 'bad eggs' are a few of the odours they can add to wine.

* gooseberry, Kiwi
**and colleagues Cabernet Franc, Merlot, Malbec, Petit Verdot

Echoes

You might find it useful to recognise, and add to, the following aroma notes in food and wine. If present in one, an echo in the other may work favourably by subtle enhancement. Or it may become too much, demanding the culinary equivalent of ear muffs.

spice/herb	black pepper (aroma, rather than heat), clove, cinnamon, vanilla, anise, mint, dill etc.
nut	almond, hazel, cashew
fruit	citrus (orange, lemon, grapefruit, lime), stone (peach, nectarine, apricot), pome (apple, quince, pear), berry (red and black), green (melon, Kiwi) etc.
vegetable	sweet hay, grass, earthy, asparagus
animal	leather, sweat, truffle, cheese, yeast, butter

Single attractive characters that match in both the food and the wine produce the most satisfactory results, for example, the truffled (or other aromatic fungus) madeira addition to rare roast beef, matched with some Cabernets or big French Burgundies. Fiddling, adding a bit of this and that, and reflecting similar notes in the glass and on the plate is exciting when you get it right. Unfortunately there are cooks who somehow manage to forget to mention a secret ingredient. Half a teaspoon of a good dry vermouth, pernod or Bourbon whisky (magic in a seafood stir-fry) or green Chartreuse, added late with the heat turned up, may just be what slipped their memory.

Flavour Couplings

Many foods 'go together'. It may be fun to make a list. Here are a few common synergisms (G) and/or balances of some fairly assertive flavours.

cheese	wine[*]
oil	vinegar
figs	ham
spinach	nutmeg
cucumber	yoghurt
steak	kidney
sausage	sauerkraut

*Too obvious to mention?

Jill Dupleix's invigorating *New Food* (Wm. Heinemann, 1994) lists 26 'flavour marriages', leading off with tomato and basil. Her feeling that "some flavours aren't interested in settling down to a life of wedded bliss. They just want to go to bed with each other" tallies nicely with my own on *exotica erotica* (1971) (see page 50).

4

Food and Wine

Tradition in the West

'History is bunk.' (Henry Ford) ... only if you don't heed it.

Albert Einstein said 'God is in the details'. The perfect union may be the result of careful attention to them. Then again a single stunning encounter could follow an impulse to taste a special wine, food or dish. For me, escape velocity is achieved with a chunk broken from the middle of a wedge of a sweet old cheese like parmesan, fresh crusty wood-fired and/or stone baked white bread made from hard wheat, and a firm red wine; finishing off with a sweet crunchy pear. Or the surprise of Yvonne Grant's match of a youthful light and fruity Cabernet with a simple salad of chicken and rocket (arugula). Freshly opened oysters with a Chablis-style white are another classic. Especially if you chomp a sprig of parsley after. They all taste so good together.

> Usually to begin dinner, there were oysters (served with the wines of Sauternes), out of whose rough, blackish Gothic shells, lined at the bottom with a patina of mother of pearl, I sipped several drops of salt water to commune with the living sea ...
>
> from Marcel Proust in *The Guermantes Way*
> (Were the wines dry?)

The centre point of the meal may be a special wine or a carefully prepared dish. It depends on your personal inclination. As a wine lover, who later became a winemaker, I tend to think about a wine first and then what food might match it. Creative chefs like Tetsuya Wakuda and Ken Hom (see 'East Meets West' on page 61) seek a wine to complement the food and develop bridges between them if necessary.

A great restaurant will have a chef with a sommelier's palate and a sommelier who understands great cuisine. A meal there will reflect these skills and the staff will be well qualified to make suggestions of suitable wines to accompany dishes on the *carte du jour*.

During the summer of '72 I was about to quit Paris after the briefest of visits and despaired of having a great meal, due to the sudden departure and the fact that many of the top places are closed during the *quinzane*. It was midday and I happened to be sitting in tourist gear outside Lucas Carton, then with two stars. I ambled over to the rather *soigné* character standing at the door and, under his dour inspection, said in my peccable French:

'Excuse me, sir. I am a visiting Australian *viticulteur* who has to return to his homeland suddenly, and it looks as though I shall be forced to leave your beautiful Paris without the blessing of a great repast. I know I am not dressed for the occasion, but could you find it in your heart to let me have a meal in your great restaurant, perhaps behind a pillar, near the dunny, whatever, please, sir?'

He looked me up and down, again, to my increasing discomfort. One is less than happy voluntarily placing oneself at a disadvantage, especially to the urban Parisian, a member of arguably the most arrogant social group on the planet.

'No,' he said, rather sadly, it seemed.

I interrupted, 'I do understand; it would have been such a treat.'

'But,' now looking me in the eye, 'if you come back at seven, when we are open ...'

I collapsed with laughter, as he did. Not many people have a loan of me. He was brilliant.

I returned to a stunning reception. Seated at a prominent table, as the evening progressed I was serviced by five professionals, from the maitre d' (it was indeed he of the delicious midday encounter), through sommelier, down. It soon became obvious why the 'barbarian' was such a hit. Because of the summer holiday break, the restaurant was only half full, with what seemed to be mainly German and Japanese tourists. Their main food and wine selections appeared to be pedestrian and unadventurous. Remember that it was nearly a quarter of a century ago. I can't recall the totality of my meal, but it began with the establishment's famous home-style sausage and a '49 Brane-Cantenac, a half bottle of which cost, I think, about ten dollars. Great restaurants of that period charged for the food and service. Great wines from their awesome cellars were available to discerning palates at what appeared to be near cost, frequently at far less than, for example, auction prices.

The sausage, poached in a stock, was formed in a light skin. Several oblique slices sat in clear demi-glace, with just a hint of madeira, the whole generously sprinkled with chopped truffle. The wine diffused a fragrance of ripe redcurrants through the room. Its flavour union with the delicate pink ham and tongue that formed the body of the 'sausage' slices was transcendental. I don't think anyone in the restaurant had ever matched the two there before, and when I sent a glass out to the kitchen for the chef, the clock virtually stopped. You can imagine the rest of the night with various members of the staff periodically clustered around my table practising our languages and food and wine ideas on each other. From the ridiculous to the sublime.

A reigning monarch of Australian gastronomy, Stephanie Alexander, has recorded this episode in *Stephanie's Seasons*, with a recipe for Duck-neck Sausage, for Max Lake. Could there ever be a food and wine match to surpass the memory of the claret and sausage of that summer's evening at Lucas Carton?

> Simplicity is the greatest mark of quality, especially when using the freshest and best ingredients that nature has to offer.
>
> Jacques Pepin

Really a simple fellow, I am a minimalist cook, using the least number of ingredients (if not amounts) and the shortest time possible to achieve results. A complicated sauce with many ingredients and long hours or even days in the preparation may not reflect the effort, unless the flavours of the constituents can be tasted. Master sauces may be the exception. Because they are so vital to great food, stocks and reductions are specifically excluded from this stricture. They have to be skimmed, defatted, and reduced. Convenient times are set apart for preparation and we keep blocks of several stocks in the freezer, on call, as it were.

This century has seen huge changes. New options now exist. There has been a swing away from saturated fats and towards complex carbohydrates, with less cooking of more vegetables. Modern food and wine production fosters flavour. Wine styles are lighter. The discipline of tradition has often been most valuable, clearly the case with great wine and food marriages of the past. The cuisines of ancient China were masterly, but certain other cultures went off the rails. The Gargantuan feasts of Imperial Rome featured a side room, the *vomitorium*. After gorging themselves on rich and tricked-up food, washed down with heavy Falernian wine, the nobles repaired to the small room, had a slave tickle the back of the throat with a feather, and were soon back at the orgy. Much later on, could those burghers really have eaten all the foods on the sideboards of seventeenth century dining halls? However gentle an art, gastronomy *is* a discipline.

Tear down the old ways, deface the walls of temples with graffiti, rebellion rules.

Ah, but have a care! The food and wine classics are easy to remember and, despite all the modern conceptions, can be comforting to fall back on (easy on the cream and butter!) in the sudden confusion and strife that are no strangers to the busy kitchen. Just for perspective, remember that most of the food eaten in the world today is eaten solely for sustenance without a thought of wine.

To give some idea of where we have come from, herewith a summary of an André Simon oration to the Australian Wine and Food Society in Melbourne, which city was, in 1971, the heart of Australian gastronomy. I was at that time already in overdrive and, encouraged by my mate Victor Gibson, pitched the tone of the address between state-of-the-art and tradition. It was an era heralded as the dawn of the second Elizabethan age, the time of the Beatles, Carnaby Street, Haight-Ashbury, the Pill, carefree sex, and nobody outside the halls of academe had even heard of cholesterol. Saturated fat implied soggy. Those yet to sin at the table questioned how a sweet sticky wine like Sauternes could match with smoked salmon or pâté, and so early in a meal.

> Today I will talk briefly about the marriage of food with wine and wine with food, because you may choose to design the repast around the food, or it may be composed for a specific great wine or wines. Contrast is a primary principle throughout life from the moment of birth; light contrasts with dark, cold with warm, dry with wet, noise with silence, chaos with rhythm. Marriages are spiced by the contrasts. Harmony and balance give pleasure. Balance in a meal is a studied achievement. In a wine it is a gift of Nature, tempered by the artistry of the winemaker.
>
> Four rich courses at a banquet infer long hours of gut wrenching indigestion. On the other hand contrasting highs with lows, and rich with piquant, leaves a pleasant memory. Choose wines in balance, where acidity and body (fruit flavour and alcohol) and tannin finish run on all fours together. That is unless you have a specific reason for doing otherwise, for example, an aggressive young Italian red with oily pasta, a perfect marriage of unequals.

The paper closed with a flourish.

> And now for the climax, the traditional marriages of wine and food, with a word on 'wild weekends', *'exotica erotica'*. Traditional marriages work with classical French and Italian food and wine. We are now thinking of *light wines with light food and heavy wines with more robust tucker.* [Mention of a few unexpectedly successful wine and food matches followed]. Apart from the smoked fish and pâté with sticky wines, how about a pop 'pearl' wine [remember them?] with Chinese roast duck, a red wine with a fish casserole with big tomato-based flavour, curry with cider, lychees or ripe white Shanghai peaches with champagne, prosciutto and melon with a sweetish iced white or rosé.

I concluded:

> The classic marriages make sense because they taste so good.
>
> White wine with white flesh.
> Red wine with darker flesh, cheese.
> Light wines, delicate food ...
> Full bodied wines, robust dishes.
> Sweet wines with sweets.
> Champagne with anything or anyone.

> The appearance of the porter and under porter with a tray covered with a snow-white cloth, which, being thrown back, displayed a pair of cold roast fowls, flanked by some potted meats and a cool salad, quickly restored his good humour. It was enhanced still further by the arrival of a bottle of excellent madeira, and another of champagne; and he soon attacked the repast with an appetite scarcely inferior to that of the medical officer.
>
> from Charles Dickens' *Martin Chuzzlewit*

Well, the address was rather provocative more than 20 years ago. That was when I had decided to give up trying to match an ordinary wine with food just because it might fit the dish. And to avoid using wine I had no conception of. The risk of mismatching 'sizes' had become obvious. I entered the realm of flavour via wine, so it followed that I often built the meal around a special wine. Then I started 'having a bash', just out of curiosity. It never killed this cat, and some great discoveries occurred. A light Pinot or Cabernet with grilled salmon and a dill dressing, and full-bodied wooded Chardonnay with veal stroganoff were thus revealed. The moral has become even clearer today: there is little reason for concern about mistakes with consenting adults in private. Have fun.

One dark night early in my first career, although not poor in the riches that reside in the heart of a close young family, we just didn't have any money. Some dull butcher's sausages (the sausages, not the butcher; Joy thought he was rather nice) appeared at the evening table. Desperate times demand desperate measures. I fetched one of the few treasures remaining from a brief period of affluence. Aside from the zip of the idea that it had probably never happened before, the snorkers really were a splendid combination with a '61 Chateau Mouton-Rothschild, which wine has since proved to be among the greatest wines of the century. To celebrate his seventieth birthday a few years ago, Lou Skinner, of Coral Gables, shared virtually all the important wines of the 1961 Bordeaux vintage with friends. A few were intrigued by my mention of this naive wine and food match.

Size and Balance — Big and Little

Size. Big/little, thick/thin, heavy/light. The word has the same implication for wine and food as it does for people or anything else. The relevance of size in wine and food marriages is now understood to be critical to the match. It was already apparent 20 years ago that unless there was some attempt to even things up, one way or the other, the result was in doubt. Rather like a chihuahua with a Great Dane.

Today we look at bridging elemental forces like FICs

and balancing flavour sizes, trying for the best matches of flavour intensity and body or 'richness' — lovely old-fashioned word; George Farwell used it a lot. Sometimes he meant cream and butter boosted, sometimes intensely flavoured, and other times both! One or the other, delicate or robust food on the plate, or wine in the glass, will guide the selection. If you are fixed on a special bottle, the size of the food is the next consideration. A particular dish will dictate the size of the accompanying wine.

Consider the sizes of certain wines and food. The spectrum of table wine extends from the most meagre Soave, Pinot Grigio (Pinot Gris and Blanc tend to be more elegantly defined), Mosel or Muscadet, thence to Chablis, the Rieslings and Traminers of Alsace, up to the heaviest white Burgundies. After rosés the light reds run from Valpolicella, various Pinot Noirs, thence via medium sized Shiraz, Spanish wines, Cabernet Sauvignons and Chianti, to great Bordeaux and Burgundies and finally Dao or Corvo. One finds that 'bubbles'[*] can be made to work with almost everything. Grossly oversimplified and truncated, this list is intended to stimulate discussion. Build your own detailed spectrum of wines, varieties and regions. *One taste of a wine is worth more than the advice of a dozen writers.*

Food flavour sizes can be briefly covered in like manner. Shellfish, flaky to oily fish, light poultry, pork, veal, big and game birds, lamb, mutton, beef, venison and other game, and so on. This refers only to the unadorned taste, not to that which has been hung too long, or has been highly sophisticated. How simple it is to slot similar sized wine (red or white) and food together, and how often it works. Should this not be the case, the FICs are the first place to look.

---

[*] Any sparkling wine, especially those of Pinot or Chardonnay.

It all depends on how deeply you wish to delve. At the fabulous Oyster Bar under the Grand Central Terminal in New York there are massive regional selections of fresh oysters and other seafoods. Particular wines may be specifically recommended for each sort of oyster, if you wish to try your palate against their experts. I have also attempted this, with equal pleasure, at the Sydney Seafood School tastings. Now that *is* finetuning to concert pitch, pretty high-powered stuff. 'Chopin', when perhaps the enjoyment might have simply been in 'Chopsticks'.

Harvey Steiman, in one of the most recent commonsensical approaches, is recommended reading for the intimidated. He is only a spit away from the 'eat and drink whatever you like together' school if the effort looks like spoiling your fun. Everyone has given up at one time or another, and had a beer or similar. *And finally, there is no substitute for experience.*

Manners

The sequence of foods and wines gives anatomy or structure to the meal. Courtney Clark tells of the chef at Government House last century who, quite overcome by the quantity, if not the quality, of the cooking wine, served a long formal French meal in reverse order.

Perhaps the single most stimulating and provocative collection of food/wine recipes and matches recently published is by David Rosengarten and Joshua Wesson. A similar message issued from the 1992 convention of the Society of Wine Educators in San Francisco, and a few months later at the *Wine Spectator*'s 'California Wine Experience'. Five principles drive today's table unions:

1. Regional matches are often made in heaven.
2. Similars work well.
3. Contrasts can lead to harmony.
4. Size is most important.
5. Personal preference remains critical.

I must say that after numerous sessions of matching wine and food over those several months, I came away confused when the FICs of wines or foods were not adequately dealt with. On another occasion, the dynamic Barbara Lang, who runs a course at the Hospitality School at Cornell University, left none of her audience in any such doubt.

Apart from Australia's impeccable Regency College in Adelaide and European schools like Anne Willan's La Varenne, Madeleine Kanman conducts one of the ultimate graduate experiences at the Beringer Vineyards in California. The tuning of dishes of great refinement with selected wines has reached an art form. She remains practical. 'When no stock is available, one can make a good sauce base by using an excellent red wine and any vegetable one cares to add to the pan. One bottle of wine takes 30 minutes to make a sauce for six.' Harvey Steiman has a mnemonic of her quick kitchen fixes of common wine/food mismatches.

> If the wine is too tannic for the food add a little salt
> If the wine is too tart, add a squeeze of lemon to the dish
> Bitter wine is confronted with a dash of bitters,
>   or citrus zest.

Food with wine is one of the gifts of European heritage. If a region produces both wine and food, a warm accommodation usually follows. Always keep this in mind should there be pressure to come up smartly with a very good meal.

A terrific field is opening up for regional wine and food celebrations, which is becoming well exploited in Australia and California. About 20 years ago Lydia Crawford and I put together one based on the bounty of North Victorian vineyard, field and stream at the Albury Hotel. The chef excelled himself. Maggie Beer, of The Pheasant Farm in the Barossa Valley, and Stephanie have recently played a similar celestial theme and variations.

Some of the ultimate food and wine experiences just seem to spring from the bounty and hospitality of a particular region in which one is travelling. Regional matches have an indefinable chemistry that on reflection starts to make sense. The things we eat taste of the things they eat, or grow in, or on. I will never forget the flavour of the prosciutto from pigs that had fed on the windfalls in a nectarine orchard at Stanthorpe. If a sheep forages on wild thyme, myrtle (what about the magical Australian lemon myrtle?), rosemary, mint or whatever, on a sparse hillside, and the bread and wine are made close by, and one is breathing the air perfumed by the sun's warming, a transcendental experience is in the making.

Ten years ago, having really no rights or qualifications to be on the high seas, except for the invitation of a friend, Joy and I mutinied off a racing yacht, to escape the perils of the mistral and the tyranny of a skipper who was an adrenalin junkie. We found ourselves cast away on a deserted beach which just happened to be a few miles north on Sardinia's Costa Smeralda. The people? Dour, almost hostile, until they saw how we enjoyed the beach and the tucker. We managed to survive on an aged sheep-milk cheese, Sardo, with huge round flat crisp thin unleavened wheat bread (*carta musica*, music paper), myrtle-scented honey, and pork fillets sprinkled with fresh herbs off the hillside and sealed over an open fire.

The wines? Just the local stuff, from grapes which every household grew and took up to the co-op when ripe, to be crushed and fermented. They would then come and collect it, take it home and bottle it in the weekend. They were drinking it within a fortnight; I mean *drinking* it. And they didn't talk about it either. Such privation!

I have already mentioned my ultra favourite, which also turns out to be a regional mix: fresh crusty bread with cheese from the middle of a wheel of aged Parmigiano, just your average grana padana, quaffed with a rough local young red. Maybe occasionally dipped in some warm free run (certified virgins are thin on the ground) olive oil. Perhaps just a slice of Parma ham from an animal with the run of an orchard's windfalls. A ripe fig? Too much!

Vigorous wine or food cultures generate appealing marriages. The quest for flavour, one of the major drives of our existence, has become enlivened by competitions that investigate the special ability of wines to match well with specific styles of food. Warren and Jacqui Mason inaugurated one such in 1982. The initial dinner was attended by many of the great 'small winemakers' of Australia. Their wines were to be paired with food of equal quality. Ten years later (and continuing to increase) an international panel adjudicated more than 800 entries in what has now become 'The Sydney International Wine Competition'. The nuptial option is now part of the assessment in many wine judging exhibitions.

Cheeses

Cheeses invite a really special wine partnership. There is something instinctively correct and appealing about cheese with wine that dwells deep in the Western mind of flavour. Perhaps it is because they are both naturally derived from the action of friendly micro-organisms on milk and fruit, products that have nourished and pleasured the human palate from the dawn of history.

There are many views on matching the flavours of wine and cheese. Among the conclusions from a recent Australian tasting, Richard Thomas and John Beeston have suggested the most successful pairings (parings?) of the new wave of fine Australian cheeses with wine, as follows: big Chardonnays with distinctive soft cheeses; lighter Chardonnays, Verdelhos, shy Pinot Noir reds and 'bubbles' with milder softer cheeses. Firm cheeses harmonised with bigger wines if they were not excessively tannic. Big whites fitted well here. The surprising, 'heavenly' marriages came from the match of liqueur Muscats with triple creams, goat cheeses, and specific blue cheeses. Californians like a Sauvignon Blanc with a goat cheese.

The answers are less clear to those cultures which have only recently taken to cheese and wine. Two Japanese authors recommend fresh cheeses like mozzarella or cream cheese with cold wines (see 'East Meets West' on page 61). Wines at room temperature are served with ripe well matured cheeses, specifically blues like Gorgonzola. The middle range wines are recommended with Brie and washed rind cheeses like Munster. Some polar contradictions emerge from their paper. These, not surprisingly, highlight the massive differences that may exist in the palate preferences of various cultures. My own Japanese friends, one living many years away from Japan, have clearly Western preferences. Despite the rapid diffusion and mixing of the ethnic cuisines that is happening as we watch, uniformity is a long way down the track, which may be all for the best.

Jesus and the Sommelier

'Why have you kept the good wine till last?' The question to the master of ceremonies at the wedding breakfast at Cana after Jesus had done his winemaking trick is as relevant now as it was 2000 years ago. Certain sequences have always made excellent flavour sense. However, the style and making of the wines have changed, and a rethink is in order.

Firstly a philosophical point. The taster, the viewer, the listener, becomes the keystone in the arch in the construction of any great art, music, painting, gastronomy, whatever. The artist invites, indeed needs, us to become part of the act of creation. In winemaking, the arch is based on the flavour of the ripe fruit, made into the best wine possible, rounded by cellaring. The keystone is the host's contribution, which includes the service of that bottle of wine, what food is eaten with it, when it is served and, most important of all, the guest's reception of it. Which is, of course, another answer to the riveting question at the end of the Cana marriage feast.

The suggested wine sequences from my primer *Start to Taste: Wine* (1984) derive from a time when lighter, fruitier wines were becoming standard. Change continues apace. Exactly ten years after this, the redoubtable Harvey Steiman is canvassing a revolutionary (not revolting!) proposal to ignore the classic wine sequences altogether. Obviously, a light white wine would be swamped by a preceding big-bodied tannic red, but we are talking here about matching wines with food, considerably less of, perhaps not even, a problem.

Most people enjoy the meal more if, when faced with the draconian choice between food and wine, a better wine is chosen, rather than a better food. Who can enjoy a meal with a poor wine?

1. Open young wines before old.* Both need air to flower.
2. Serve dry wine before sweet. It is difficult to enjoy the reverse.*
3. Take light before full bodied wine, or the lesser gets lost.
4. Sparkling wines cold, white cool, and red about room temperature.
5. Enjoy all wine, but don't babble about ordinary bottles. Respect the best wines.

In 1959 I assembled 24 mature Coonawarra red wines, now generally accepted as the most consistent of the classic Australian winegrowing areas, but virtually unsung in the year of this tasting. Tony Nelson's (winemaster of Woodleys) subsequent thanks for my efforts took the form of a dinner featuring Coonawarra reds up to 30 years old. That was a revelation! Jimmy Watson had showed me several of the wines on different occasions, many made by Bill Redman, but there was never a collection like this, before or since. They were served in what appeared to be a random order. An old wine, then a far younger one, all over the place. As the evening flowed on, the pattern clarified. A dazzling exercise. We were in the hands of a grand master, with the sequence dictated by the size of the wine flavours of different years, and the foods he had selected to go with them. The *tour de maître*, the most instructive focus of an unforgettable experience, was when the oldest wine was opened and decanted. The dish that it was to accompany was already on the

---

* These are not inviolable rules.

table before us. The wine was enjoyed at is peak. Half an hour later it had fallen apart. All the wines were opened at different times, some much earlier in the day, ensuring they came on the table at their best. Tony had actually been associated with the making of every wine served that evening. So this incredible performance was based on vast experience and a fantastic palate. The food matches were equally stunning. I have often made good use of his conception of cold sliced roast duck breast set in a dark Morella cherry glaze. Perfection at the table is rare and this experience of it is worth recalling as an ultimate statement on the sequence of wine service. Tony and Jesus may well agree.

East Meets West

Richard Hosking tells us that there is a Shinto kitchen god of the cooking fire and stove, Kojin Sama. He is rather fierce and if your efforts do not meet with his approval, he burns the kitchen down.

The study and teaching of flavour is a continual learning process. These days, I find I am doing a lot more teaching and a lot less learning. Who was it said you can't learn while you are talking? Which may help explain why of more recent times, progress has been glacial. Perhaps the main reason may be that there really have not been a lot of original thinkers and teachers on the subject of this book. Several are acknowledged and quoted in these pages. In my experience, among the most impressive of those able to thread their way through the maze of the FICs of the table wines of the world, and those of challenging Oriental foods, one finds ethnic Japanese or Chinese with really finetuned palates, who also have developed a love of dry white and red wines.

Australia has a few of these culinary geniuses, the most impressive of whom, to the author, is Tetsuya Wakuda of Sydney. As a sole practitioner for the past eight years, he just seems to get better and better. His fans were quietly convinced of the award of 'Restaurant of the Year, 1993' long before the final event. His craft is the ultimate declaration of the quality of foods of the season. He has been heard to whisper 'everything comes to Sydney'. An important reason for mentioning him here is a highly tuned palate that justifies the strength of his claim (rare in one so unassuming) that he delights in planning dishes around a special wine offered by a client. The more complex ('difficult') it is, the more satisfying is a happy result to the challenge.

Ken Hom is very much into matching Oriental food and Western wine. One of the driving forces of his East/West fusion cooking arose from his love of the wines, and modifying Chinese dishes to accompany them. Having learnt much from his cooking, I recently listened to him philosophising that the spirit of the chef is in the food on the plate, even when its creator is absent. My mind flew back 30 years to the first time I tasted the wine of a certain winemaker. In an abstract way, its resemblance to her (all negatives, *une belle dame sans merci*) was eerie, as though the body of the wine had arisen from her very essence. This was the first time that the idea of a certain transference of the maker's soul to the product was so forcefully delivered. Completely agreeing with Ken Hom, I occasionally amuse myself by pondering the warmth, or otherwise, of the winemaker, in terms of the style of the wine itself. There is more in it than might be apparent. There is a corollary to this spiritual association with wine and food. The most creative young chefs don't seem to mind if they are not wildly successful commercially, as long as they are appreciated and, in the words of Hilary Wright, 'able to practice their passion'.

The Japanese are taking more wine with food. I first visited Tokyo in 1968, to find a mere handful of wines on the shelves of the grand department stores. In 1984 there were 40, not including a large, locked, air-conditioned glass cabinet of very expensive treasures. Now there are many times this number. Well into this century, the Japanese diet consisted almost totally of the produce of the home islands and included rice, greens, fish, pork and poultry. Sake, brewed from rice, was the preferred tipple. Richard Hosking has much to offer on this subject.

Two Japanese technologists (Wantanabe and Fujiwara, 1990) have undertaken a 'new consideration of the compatibility of wine and cuisine'. And once again the baby is in danger of disappearing with the bath water. Some of their illuminations are important, for example, the wine's temperature having the ability to mask or increase the effects of acid, sweetness and tannin on the palate. They proffer flat statements of 'Wine-Cuisine Compatibility' from their surveys of Japanese food and world wines. For anyone involved in catering to Japanese guests it could represent state of the art in perhaps the most mobile culture in the world today. Briefly summarised, their principles include the following.

Most wines or wine styles are grouped according to three temperature categories, to be served at 5 (fridge temperature), 12, and 20 (Japanese room temperature) degrees centigrade. Examples are champagne, sweet German wines and Cabernet Sauvignon, respectively. The 'wine will taste better' served closer to the recommended temperature. Sweet wine cold, and tannic wines warmer. Traditional enough, so far.

The acids in wine form the next grouping and are linked with secondary bacterial effects on wine flavour. They fall into service at the three temperature categories. Still with it? This acid grouping is a new concept. It is based on the increase of lactic acid and the bitter flavours, 'which develop after the death of living organisms'. This could be appropriate to the consumption of raw fish and so on and the temperature of wine service. The match with wine flavours is, to say the least, far out. Why not a selection from the vast age and quality range of sake in this context?

Fish and meat are classified by low or high fat component. Venison fillet as low fat, and marbled sirloin as high fat are not controversial, nor is the seasonal variation in the fat of individual seafood groups. What does one make of their recommendations for the low fat groups with cold wines, and the high fat groups with wines at room temperature?

The vegetable section is even further removed from the Western palate. The cold wine group goes with fresh, boiled or salad vegetables, but the chilli, garlic, salt pickled vegetables in the *kim chee* style, which I adore, overwhelm the palate, so that not a single wine can even be tasted, let alone enjoyed, despite their recommendation. Most would agree with their position on FICs in the handling of 'spices and seasonings'. They recommend that 'seasonings are effective to make wine and food compatible, especially when the components in the food do not go well with the wine'. Which brings us to the final section of this book, flavour bridges.

PART THREE

MATCHING FOOD AND WINE

5

Flavour Bridges

Cooking with Wine

> Dinner is not what you do in the evening before something else. Dinner is the evening.
>
> Art Buchwald

I am with those who baulk at using expensive wine in cooking (that is, except for an occasional splash, for a benediction, just before serving the food with that wine). Anyhow, I would sooner put it in the chef than the dish. No, the whole point is that the finesse of great wine is almost always completely lost in such a translation. Cooking wine has to be drinkable, and then it has myriad uses: marinades, stocks, stews, sauces, essences and so on. A lot used early and reduced in the cooking, or a little added late, but in time to blow off the alcohol. Once heat is used several things happen. The alcohol evaporates, which is good, avoiding an odd flavour if it persists. Wines get sweeter, and more acid. This acidity throws more dishes out of balance than almost any other FIC, mainly because it may not have been anticipated. Madeleine Kanman's quick fixes are listed on page 55.

Flambé and barbecue foods are fun, and the Maillard and brown caramel boost is sensational. Drizzling a bit of wine or spirit on food on a grill, near completion of its cooking time, is another excellent bridge. There is more, in 'Manners' on page 54.

The Chef/Sommelier's Brain in Action

> Your father insists on asking an awkward question: 'What does he want? If he wants to drink at meals, he would want white wine, but then he couldn't drink Spanish wine, then it is to drink with dessert, but then what does he drink with the main course? This must be resolved before we send anything.'
>
> Mother's letter to Marcel Proust, 1890

My first encounter of that 'improbability', a red wine with fresh white fish, was at Beppi's in Sydney 30 years ago. Fresh poached schnapper doused in the big flavours of a tomato, wine and onion sauce, with capers, Livornese style, I think. It was a marvellous match with a medium bodied red. A gate opened and I crossed over.

Additions, from simple to vastly complex, bridge the seemingly impossible. Some verge on creative genius, which you may remember is one per cent inspiration and the rest hard work. There are some wild cards in the form of unexpected masking (G) or synergism (G). The degree of alcohol may be a problem. Salty foods (e.g. ham) can lend a bitter tone to high alcohol wines. Delicate dishes that are overwhelmed by astringent wines may be rescued by a touch of salt. Sweetness in foods makes a tart wine taste even more unbalanced. Acid foods taste less so with acidic wine and, despite what has been said about the difficulties of such an addition, a light vinaigrette may save the day. Low acid, flat flavoured wines are difficult to match with any food. If the wine has lingering sweetness, the dish needs its own sweetness from fruit, honey, even an added sweet wine. Daryl Corti has a beauty: drizzling maple syrup or honey over a ripe

Gorgonzola, plus a big Barolo. Some Italians take Barolo with everything (do they jest?), but if you appreciate the concept of 'head food' you will understand why I wish Daryl the best of luck. I will not be drawn into the Cabernet/chocolate debate. Port and chocolates marry beautifully, worse luck for the calorie conscious. I am a light eater. As soon as it's light, I start to eat. There are some odd cross-clashes. You can't match a 'sticky' with salt (e.g. caviar). Artichokes have a sweetness booster in their flavour and are tricky to match with any but a tart wine.

Ethnic food from cultures which tend not to take alcohol at table are notorious for the manner in which their FICs annihilate Western wine flavours. In many authentic Chinese restaurants older diners take neat whisky or brandy, with three to four times the alcohol content of table wines. [Later you will see how a highly refined flavour bridge can mend the rift.] Traditional Japanese foods had few FICs until the latter half of this century.

Deglazing a pan with the wine to be served (or similar) is an excellent flavour bridge from the cooked food to that wine. Deglazing a barbecue or mustard sauce with wine makes a similar bridge. The regional French development of this theme is the classic Entrecôte, a beefsteak sirloin sent to the table with a reduced wine sauce, accompanied by a bottle of the wine of the region (or something close to it) that was used in the sauce. In Bordeaux it is called Bordelaise, and in Burgundy, Marchand de Vin, and never the twain shall meet. The visitor is amused at the rivalry between the two regions and in the way they used to ignore each other, despite the fact that, in this case, they use exactly the same method to marry their food and wine.

Mother Sauces and a Master Sauce

Elizabeth David, MFK Fisher, and Julia Child and collaborators were among those who led many of the post-World War II generation out of the culinary wilderness. Wallace Irwin's *Garrulous Gourmet* and Ted Moloney's *Oh for a French Wife* had much the same influence in Australia, perhaps an even more important one because there was no traditional and very little ethnic background on which to build. And those individuals who were to lead Australia to its current excellence in food and wine at the table were but frowns on parental brows, more or less. It was obligatory for every aspiring cook to master the French classic mother sauces. They and their numerous offspring are now yielding to lighter dressings. Charles Saunders lists five: salsas, chutneys, marmalades, purées, and coulis. The perspective widens. Natural stock reductions remain paramount, rarely with a little added beurre blanc or a fine starch (e.g. arrowroot or corn) to give some body or smoothness. Yoghurt, tofu, vinaigrettes with infused oils, and flavoured vinegars are state of the art now.

A note of caution. While stock reductions are admirable flavour bridges from food to wine, salsas can be too dramatic, and the tartness of the vinaigrette may dominate. Olive oil connects with Sauvignon Blanc or Semillon, calming a green flavour which is always lurking there. Specific fruit flavours in wine are critical to the matching of similar notes in food. John Thomas constructs a stunning bridge between a rich poultry confit and a fine red Burgundy, with a marmalade of beetroot, veal stock, thyme and orange juice.

Beetroot marmalade (for 30 plates)

beetroot	*8 'matchsticked', parboiled*
veal stock	*1 litre*
butter	*600 grams*
fresh thyme	*2 tablespoons*
juice	*6 oranges*

Simmer for 1½ hours, stirring to stop it sticking, until it turns to jam. Keeps for days in the fridge.

Irma Power's master sauce is an excellent example of a master stroke to unite the difficult FICs in food of the East with wine of the West. It is offered here as the ultimate professional way to go. It starts:

soya sauce, Kikkoman standard medium	*1 part*
duck stock	*5 parts*
Sauvignon Blanc	*5 parts*

five spices, enough to taste, individualise it yourself
fresh ginger, ditto
white sugar, ditto
dried orange peel, ditto
star anise, ditto (repetition of a five spice note is acknowledged)

Simmer and reduce to two-thirds.

This master sauce is used on one occasion during the two day preparation, later with a tiny cornstarch addition for glaze, as the final dressing of thrice cooked pigeon, served on a bed of dried lily flowers, Peking dried mushrooms and lightly sauteed white onion, which have also had a basic stock poaching. That complex preparation was presented (and married exquisitely) with a medium bodied 1986 Beringer Cabernet Sauvignon bottled in Imperials. Obviously beyond the reach of all but the most dedicated amateur, this exercise has been described to illustrate the epitome of finetuning of the FICs in food and wine.

Another unexpected tour de force took the form of a dinner by Cynthia and Ted Jackson, with Manuel Damien, at the Little Snail, for the visit of Alexandre and Beranger sur Laluces of Chateau d'Yquem. Different sized years of the sweet wines of the chateau were served with every course. These wines were used as ingredients in the flavour bridges that married the food celebrants except for two courses, a rich pâté and the dessert, when the wines themselves accompanied the food. Everything worked well. Not a meal to be undertaken too often, but a great exercise in flavour principles. For some, 'bubbles' all through the meal carries the day nicely, the acidity, mild fruit flavour, and a non-lingering sweetness favouring easy matches.

> It is very poor consolation to be told that a man who has given one a bad dinner, or a poor wine, is irreproachable in private life.
>
> who else but Oscar Wilde

Some of the most exciting food and wine is now to be seen in brasseries and smaller restaurants, the product of inspired youthful chefs, who are often more than kitchen cobbers (G). The feeling they have for FICs is something to aim for. There is nothing to stop you getting up early and going to the markets like they do, thereby achieving the perfection of simplicity. And matching the size or 'weight' of the food and wine. Most of those who like to play 'chopsticks' have little wish to become concert pianists. Just having some idea of the efforts and talent of the professional enhances appreciation. Thus it is with flavour. Don't let its pursuit turn you off. Sharing at the table is the real pleasure.

CODA

6

Gastronomy:
The Art of Flavour

Since Eve ate apples, much depends on dinner.
Lord George Byron (Don Juan)

Gastronomy, 'the art and science of good eating',[*] is truly an art form, and its principles transmute to a philosophy. Under the banner of flavour, all *amateurs* of life, the student at a food school, the caring host and hostess, the market throng, the apprentice chef, the technologist, move easily into gastronomy and the art of flavour.

There are those who consider that home cooking is the best cooking. On all fours with this, many would agree with Patience Gray (*Honey from a Weed*) that it is the countryman who is the real gourmet. 'It is he who has cultivated, raised, hunted or fished the raw materials and has made the wine himself.' Others take the opposite view that such food implies a second rate culture and that housewives (and their spouses) can't achieve serious results. I don't think the two conceptions are mutually exclusive, merely that one excels in cooking for six or so and the professional burnishes a larger quantity, for 60, to an art form.

Flavour has achieved a high status more than once in history. Perhaps the first pinnacle of the practice of 'the art and science of good eating' was described by

---

[*] *Oxford English Dictionary.*

Athenaeus in about A.D. 228 in his fantasy of a three day banquet. His classic, *The Deipnosophists* [philosophers at dinner], is a witty and erudite parody, a grab bag of gossip, as well as an encyclopaedia of foods, wines, and table practice and manners, one of the ultimate source books of gastronomy for nearly half the human record.

The seven volumes of Charles Gulick's English translation outline the form that the ideal repast might have taken. Discussion of the quality and selection of the wine, food and music continue throughout the symposium to which the table talk of the feast transmutes. That form would be instantly familiar to anyone attending one of the numerous gatherings of foodies worldwide. As would the maitre d's plan of the wine and food sequence at the wedding reception at Cana, that which Jesus interrupted by producing the best wine last. What would He have thought of the Greek ideal, with dinner first, then the wines, and then formal discussion?

The next classical peak, that of the Florentine Renaissance, migrated to flourish yet again at the French court. The musings of the decidedly odd Grimod de la Reyniére in the French Revolution are a landmark. The state of the art was later defined by an analytical judge and professional musician, Dr Jean-Anthelme Brillat-Savarin. His three works, *Physiologie du Gout*, *Les Classiques de la Table* and *Méditations Gastronomique*, dominated the subject for much of the century past. Here, in his own words, are his 12 precepts for a gastronomic repast:

1. Let the number of guests not exceed twelve, so that the conversation may be constantly general.
2. Let them be chosen so that their occupations are various, their tastes are analogous, and with such points of contact that there will be no need for the odious formality of introductions.

3. Let the dining room be brilliantly lit, the cloth spotless, and the atmosphere at a temperature of from 60 to 68 degrees Fahrenheit.
4. Let the men have wit without pretension and the women be pleasant without being coquettes.
5. Let the dishes be exceedingly choice, but small in number; the wines of first quality, each in its degree.
6. Let the order of serving be from the more substantial dishes to those that are lighter; and from the simpler wines to those of finer flavour.
7. Let the eating proceed without hurry or bustle, since the dinner is the last business of the day; and let the guests look upon themselves as travellers about to reach the same destination together.
8. Let the coffee be hot and the liqueurs chosen with particular care.
9. Let the drawing room to which the guests retire be large enough to admit a game of cards for those who cannot do without it, while leaving ample scope for after-dinner chat.
10. Let the guests be detained by the social enjoyment, and animated by the hope that, before the evening is over, there is still some pleasure in store.
11. Let the tea be not too strong, the toast artistically buttered, and the punch skilfully made.
12. Let nobody leave before 11 o'clock and everybody be in bed by 12.

André Simon, friend and inspiration, was very old when we first met. His wine and food matches followed the classic pattern with few exceptions. I did not know him to be adventurous. He taught us there was always something new to learn. At dinner on one occasion, his niece asked for some butter when the cheese plate appeared on the table. 'One does not take butter with cheese, my dear,' he politely informed her. 'But,' she said, 'the butter is not for my cheese, it is for my biscuit.' I was deeply honoured to give the André Simon Oration of the International Wine and Food Society at Singapore in 1988. Titled 'The Excitement of Wine', it explored the subject of the sexual pheromones in wine. Having spent several weeks in his company, I think he would have approved.

Challenged by the gastronomic principles of more than a century ago, I wonder how future readers will receive a contemporary set of principles of the pleasures and lore of the table:

1. Know and understand your own senses, particularly those involved with flavour perception (discussed in the first section of this work).
2. Moderation and restraint must become instinctive.
3. Consideration and good manners are as important now as they have always been.
4. Pleasant matching of company and surroundings, possibly including soft music should it suit the taste of guests.
5. Presentation of food and wine at an artistic table, both to be statements of the style of the house.
6. Highest quality food. This most emphatically does not mean that it has to be costly.
7. The better the wine, the better the food tastes.
8. Balance, above all; not a series of fat foods.
9. Contrast on the plate, and in the courses.
10. The end of the meal should be as carefully planned as the start. To conclude with sweetness is one certain way to feel good then and next day.

Contrast and variety are biologically certifiable culinary principles.

Harold McGee

Food Options

A game involving guesstimates can be great fun at the table and, if well organised, can be a most instructive exercise. Matching wits and knowledge in competing to guess the origin, method of preparation and so on of food, wine and incense (then called Kodo) dates back at least to the eighth century A.D. in Japan and the second century in Rome. Ted Davis and his colleagues in the NSW Wine and Food Society have evolved one of the great gastronomic experiences. Briefly, a secret *ménu dégustation* is prepared by non-participating selfless members, accompanied by a polysampling questionnaire. Under the supervision of a good master of ceremonies, tables of eight compete with vigour, and the hilarity sits well with gastronomy. Principles numbers 2 and 3 above take a bit of a hammering, but number 10 makes up for them.

The great gastronomic experiences grow from an integration of the senses. The people, the appearances of food and wine on the table, conversation, background music, the aromas, all combine to enhance each sense singly. Physiologically, at this time, taste and smell appear to be particularly subject to melding with seeing, hearing, and touching.

There is an intersensory phenomenon that may possess guests on such occasions. *Synesthesia* is something like a short circuit in the wiring of the brain, for example, 'colour-hearing', when specific sounds evoke the actual experience of certain colours. This is not uncommon in musicians. Words may evoke colours, sounds, perhaps in those poetically inclined. Scarcely audible music of the Baroque may enhance flavour perception and who knows what else.

This book concludes with a true story that, naturally, has a moral. Brillat-Savarin was always referring to a man he admired, a M de Borose. He led off one of his magna opera with a quote from his work.

> Gastronomy is nothing but a combination of reflection, to appreciate, with science, to make perfect.

A great practitioner of the art, M de Borose was spending the day enjoying himself in his usual fashion in the company of friends, on this occasion out in the country. The closing quotation is from the good doctor.

> It was one of those unseasonably warm days, a forerunner of spring, ... when the sky suddenly became gloomy, and a frightful storm burst forth, with thunder, rain and hail. M de Borose sought shelter under a poplar whose branches seemed to offer some protection.
>
> Ill-fated shelter! The tree's lofty top rose to the clouds as if to find the electric fluid and the rain falling on the branches served as its conductor. Suddenly a fearful explosion was heard, and the unfortunate pleasure-seeker fell dead without having time to breathe a sigh.

It is later than you think.

APPENDIX

Table 1 Odour Classification

aldehydic	sweaty, beansprouts
animal	musk, skatole
balsamic	vanilla, cinnamon
camphor	
citrus	orange, lemon
earthy	
fatty	tallow, animal fat
floral	various flowers
fruity	various fruits
green	fresh cut grass
medicinal	lysol, phenol
metallic	
minty	
mossy	forest floor, seaweed
powdery	baby powder
resinous	tree gums
spicy	cloves, pepper, mace
woody	oak, cedar

Animal, vegetable and mineral will do, if this list is intimidating.

The human sexual pheromones (G) have been around for hundreds of millions of years, but they waited for John Amoore to come along and list them:

musky	androstenone*
spermous	pyrroline
cheesy	isovaleric acid (IVA)
fishy	triethylamine (TMA)*
milky, hint of butter	isobutyraldehyde

*These exert a disproportionate flavour impact in foods. (See 'Sex, Again. The Sexual Pheromones' on page 39 and also the Glossary.)

Table 2 Pheromone Analogues in Food and Wine
(from *Start to Taste: People*, 1985)

A provisional list for discussion.

Wine

Cabernet Sauvignon, aged	androstenone
new wood flavour in wines (red and white)	"
madeira	"
champagne	IVA, pyrroline
some Pinot, Chardonnay, Riesling	sweaty

Food

truffles*	androstenone
boarmeat	"
parsley, celery, carrot tops	"
arugula, rocket	vaguely androstenone
green coriander	"
asparagus	suggestive
chestnuts, roast, boiled or glace	pyrroline
persimmon, ripe	"
corn on the cob	"
soft cheeses	IVA
caviar	fresh marine
oysters	"
anchovies	TMA
prawn, oyster, fish, sauces	"
malted milk, some cheeses	IBA, IVA
vanilla**	

* 'The truffle is not a positive aphrodisiac, but it can, in certain situations, make women more tender and men more agreeable.' - Harold McGee.

** Vanilla is the oxidised form of the sexual pheromone that works for nematode worms. In their case it derives from rotting wood, which is not so different from the way that oak contributes to truffles, and to the flavour of wines matured in new oak barrels. Some regions, like the forests of Limousin, lend a marked vanilla note to oak. Cabernet makes its own pheromonal contribution as the wine matures.

Table 3 Relative Sweetness (part after Coultate)

Taking table sugar (sucrose) one unit as the standard.

glucose	0.42
lactose (milk sugar)	0.19
cyclamate	30.00
Nutrasweet (TM) [Aspartame]	200.00
saccharin	300.00

Saccharin is picked up at 1/700 the amount of sucrose; about half of the population perceive it as bitter.

Table 4 Reducing Sugar, as grams per litre

A wine is said to taste bone dry if it tests less than 0.5.

dry	about 2
touch of sweetness	7
sweet, lingering	10+
very sweet ('sticky')	20+

Table 5   Relative Sourness, as pH* (part after Rietsz)

lime juice	1.9
vinegar (average)	2.8
wine (average)	3.4
tomato	4.2
beer	4.5
coffee	5.0
milk	6.9
water	7.0

*pH is a scale with a ten times difference between each unit. 7 is neutral, neither acid nor alkaline. Lime juice is among the most acid of natural tastes.

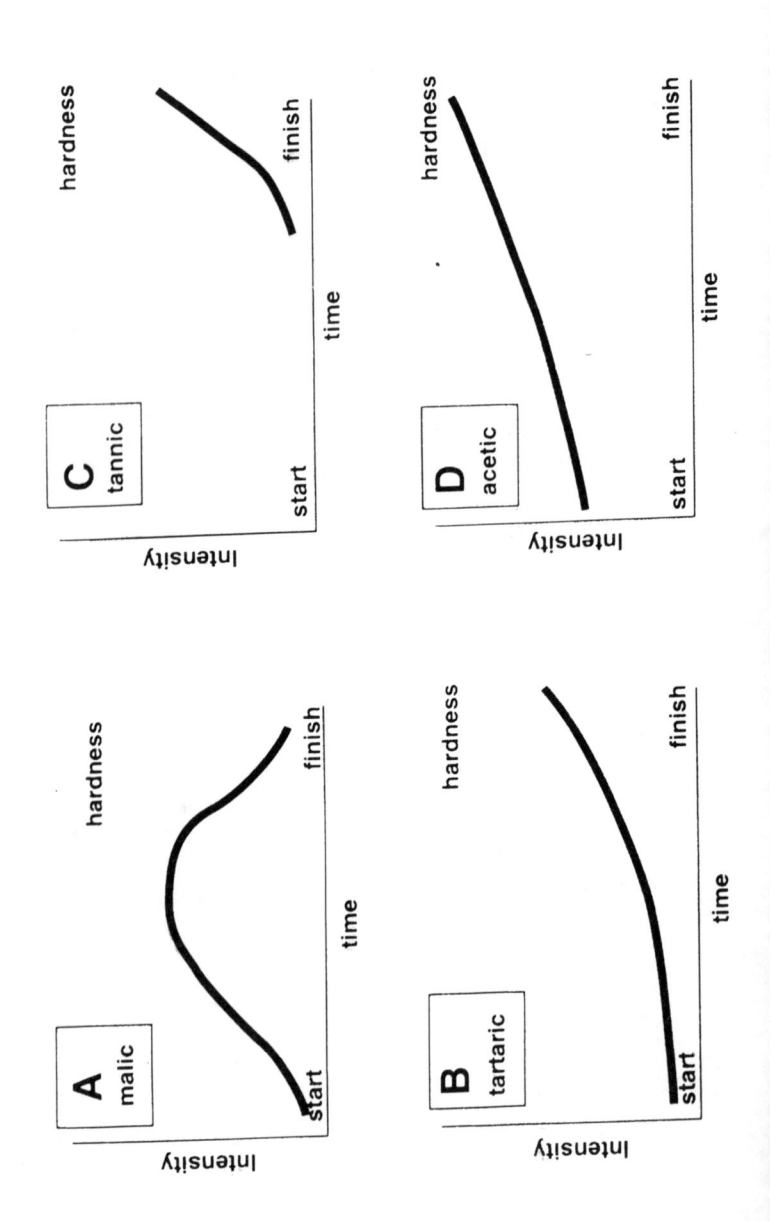

APPENDIX

A malic

B tartaric

C tannic

D acetic

Figure 1 Wine Acids and Palate Length

Acidity lifts all flavour, and wine is no exception. Low acid wines taste flat and mawkish. The four acids shown are those most commonly found in wine, although acetic acid in more than small amounts is an indication of spoilage. The graphs can easily be verified by tasting these acids at the levels they normally exist in wine (see 'The Eye Gets the Upper Hand' on page 23).

Perhaps the most important principle illustrated is the idea of *palate length*, the time taken for the flavour impact to register and then either to fall away, as in the example of malic acid (A), or to persist as the *aftertaste*, particularly in the case of tannins (C) and acetic acid (D). The persistence of tartaric acid (B) is brief, and adds much of the 'flintiness' of classical Chablis. The grip of tannin can be hard, or quite velvety, depending on the amount present, and the age of the wine. The hardness of acetic acid is unique, asserting itself long before its vinegar aroma can be picked up in the wine. The hard grip of an aged red wine is due to the combined effect of whatever acetic acid may be present and chemical changes in the structure of the tannins. It signifies that the wine has nowhere to go, that not even the most optimistic cellarer can expect any improvement.

90　　　　　　　　　　APPENDIX

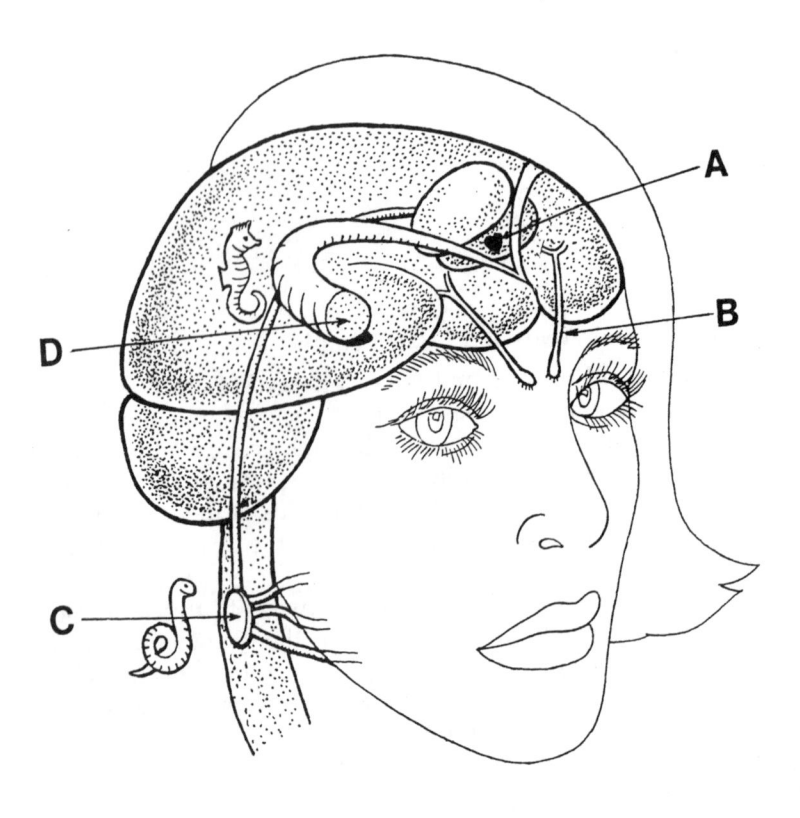

Figure 2 A Whimsical Depiction of the Brain of Flavour

A. The heart symbol represents the emotional drives that reside in the clumps of neurones that form the hypothalamus. Hunger and sexuality are but two of these. The hypothalamus and its links are the heart of the limbic system, a loose concept of that old, deeply hidden part of the brain which is now becoming recognised to be half of a working entity with the new cerebral cortex, with which it has massive connections.

B. Olfactory nerves which carry the information from odour sensors at the top of the back of the nasal cavity. They pass directly to the smell brain. All other flavour information relays through the thalamus. There is some merit in the idea that the thinking cortex developed from the olfactory input of our evolutionary past. We are, because we smell.

C. The taste brain in the medulla. The worm has been selected as an evolutionary model of this most primitive of the centres of sensory inputs (sour, salty, umami, sweet and bitter) that regulate the health of all living cells. It is called the solitary nucleus, and with its tract makes its way to the thalamus. It is fed by three cranial nerves and is the first relay from sensors in the mouth, tongue and throat. It lives beside the life support centres for breathing, the heart and, appropriately, the centre for rejection of food by vomiting. Other tastes are discussed in 'Taste Geography' on page 14.

D. The smell brain. The point of the arrow shows the amygdala (almond) and the graceful curved structure (passing forwards from deep in the temporal lobe of the cortex) is called the hippocampus, from its fancied resemblance to a seahorse. These two are endowed with quite a range of involvements, from memory to olfaction, and are among the richest of the sources of the happy hormones, as I choose to call endorphins in this context.

Any depiction of the idea of flavour must encompass the dominance of sight, and the way food and wine are presented at the table. This is discussed in 'The Eye Gets the Upper Hand' on page 23.

Glossary*

androstenone Principal male pheromone. Females secrete it in lesser amounts. Secreted by apocrine glands in most of the hair bearing areas. This fascinating subject is discussed at length in *Fragrances of Love* (unpublished as yet). Odour variously described as honey, urine, stale socks, musk and more. Great Cabernet and some other oak driven wines have a perceptible androstenone note, as does celery and so on (see Table 2, 'Pheromone Analogues in Food and Wine', on page 84). Half of the human male population is 'odour blind' to it, and about one-third of females. Training can improve these figures.

cobber Oz slang for mate, buddy.

cockie Oz slang for farmer, grower. As in wheat cockie, sheep cockie.

endorphins Neurotransmitters (G) released in quantity by specific areas of the smell brain. These 'happy hormones' are natural pain killers. They are found all over the body; for example, there is a high concentration in the placenta and in breast milk, and they cause contraction of the muscle of the vas deferens. (See also Figure 2, 'A Whimsical Depiction of the Brain of Flavour', on page 91.)

---

* Also refer to Index.

embryo The early human embryo reruns the evolutionary models of which the baby is the finished product, squalling and cheesy straight off the showroom floor. At four to eight weeks, a pouch grows up from the back of the nose to fuse with a stalk coming down from the hypothalamic area of the brain stem. This pituitary pouch will later come to 'taste' and respond to chemicals in the circulation. Up to the age of four months, the human embryo has a vomeronasal system, during the reprises of the fish/frog/reptile brains. Remnants may remain.

glutamate The amino acid glutamine exists in quantity in the body during digestion of protein food. Its monosodium salt MSG has the umami taste (meaty, brothy) and is widely added to food as a flavour enhancer. It may also act as a neurotransmitter.

gutsier tucker If you ever visit Australia, you might find this outback. From guts, strength, and tucker, food.

hedonic rating 'Like it, don't like it' or 'yum, yuk' in the case of children, expressed as a numerical scale.

isomers Molecules of the same composition and weight, but differing in physical or chemical properties. There are several kinds. The young Louis Pasteur spent innumerable nights peering down a polarising microscope, laboriously separating by hand those crystals which rotated light to the left from those which rotated it to the right (stereo-isomerism).

IVA Isovaleric acid, one of the principal female pheromones; acidy, with light cheesy notes.

masking Just what it says, obscuring one flavour by one or more others. 1+1+1=2.

MIP (or IMP) See pyrazine.

neurotransmitter At least 50 chemicals have been identified in the juice between the end of one nerve and the start of another. The transfer of electrical impulses between the two is effected by chemicals moving across this synaptic gap. [Conversely, they may inhibit the further transmission of an impulse.] A single neuron may secrete several of them. It all seems rather cumbersome. It appears that pheromones, hormones, and emotions have all at one time or another got a little confused about their roles in this microscopic interval. I gave an address to the Royal Australian Chemical Institute (1992, unpublished) on a direct evolutionary sequence from aroma to emotion, where discussing the possibility of each neurotransmitter defining a human emotion elicited a couple of job offers from the audience.

pheromone Peter Karlson and Martin Luscher coined this from two Greek words to indicate a chemical message between two members of the same species. Pheromones travel in air or water. They may attract or repel, stimulate or inhibit. It is often easier to observe their effects (e.g. in domestic animals) than to describe them. Bees may respond to 30 different messages. The Queen's (bee!) pheromone has ten such.

postcentral gyrus A final major flavour relay station in the newest brain cortex.

pyrazine A molecule based on a six atom nucleus, of which nitrogen donates a north and a south pole, and carbons form the rest of the ring. Pyrazines are one of the major branches of flavour chemistry, wherein the 'green' flavours reside. (MIP or IMP is a major part of the capsicum/bell pepper aroma.) Some of humankind's favourites: toasty-roasty, coffee, chocolate and so many others.

synergism The net effect is greater than the simple sum of the ingredients. 1+1=3.

thalamus Major relay station for body sensation, at the top of the brain stem. Crude impressions are then fine-tuned in the overlying cerebral cortex. It squats over the hypothalamus. Smell messages relay direct to the smell brain, with no thalamic intervention.

TMA The menstrual pheromone. Lightest and most volatile of all the pheromones, it is among the most ancient and potent of all food flavourings, rivalling MSG in its flavour power. Derived from anchovies, fish sauces, and rotting prawns, it is available at any Asian deli as blachan. In amounts of any more than at a scarcely perceptible threshold, when it is at its most attractive, it can be a turn-off to both sexes. It is the classic example of perhaps the most fundamental of all flavour principles, LESS IS MORE.

trigeminal Fifth cranial nerve. It relays all sensation (excepting smell and the quintet of the solitary nucleus) from the head and neck to the cortex via the thalamus.

Biographical Notes

Beppi's Long established top-flight classical Italian restaurant and cellar, Sydney.

Beeston, John Wine authority, co-founder of Brokenwood, the Hunter Valley vineyard.

Beer, Maggie Barossa Valley-based gourmet food producer, gastronome, author. Founded 'The Pheasant Farm', where her table illustrated an inspired union of local products.

Bohdan, Tony Chef for the Friday table at the Chevron Hotel, Sydney, during the Frank Christie era, when Len Evans was beverage manager. Now *that* was a synergism.

Buttery, Ron World authority on pyrazines (G); an Australian researching out of Berkley, California.

Clark, Courtney Consultant to the food industry, multi-media personality.

Clarke, Oz London-based wine judge, prolific and iconoclastic writer. The awesome accuracy of his palate appears not to have been affected by singing the male lead in *Evita* some years ago.

Corti, Daryl Co-judge at the Los Angeles County Fair, wine merchant, respected foodie.

Crawford, Lydia Formerly chatelaine of Mount Annan, near Albury, NSW. A direct descendant of one of

Australia's first wine families, the Reynells, her connoisseurship and table are a delight. Andrew Caillard MW of Sydney is a grandson.

David, Elizabeth Doyenne of writers on food, in English, after World War II. Not the least remembered for first employing (and influencing) that adornment of the world of wine, Hugh Johnson.

Davis, Ted Past president, NSW Wine and Food Society, the only branch in the world to hold a weekly function. Began the Food Options caper that has been so much fun and so educational for members and their guests.

Damien, Manuel His Sydney restaurant 'The Little Snail' at Bondi, with Cynthia Jackson as manager, was an early Australian/French Sydney restaurant of very high class. Now at Forster, NSW.

Farwell, George George and Noni Farwell. He, distinguished Australian author. She, one-time editorial staff member of *The Australian Women's Weekly*. They did much to advance the Lake family palate.

Gibson, Victor Honoured first president of the Wine and Food Society of Australia (1969–71). Unforgettable friend, I was never able to thank him for his bequest of a case of '75 Beychevelle.

Grant, Yvonne Chef, gourmet, author, epitome of style.

Hom, Ken Chinese derivative-style chef, influential philosopher, teacher and writer.

Hosking, Richard Professor of Cultural Anthropology, Shido University, Hiroshima. Leading authority, in English, on the food philosophy of Japan, founding member of the Hiroshima Champagne Society (four members) and a classy harpsichordist.

Jackson, Cynthia See Manuel Damien.

Joseph, Robert International wine judge, editor of *Wine* magazine.

Levy, Paul Distinguished author, international food and wine authority, television producer, warm host. The anecdote on page 25 is from *Out to Lunch*.

Mason, Warren President of the Asian Pacific Zone of the International Wine and Food Society. Catering consultant. With Jacqui, his wife, they have been in the vanguard of the study of matching wine and food, more recently as an integral part of their now well recognised Sydney International Wine Competition.

Moloney, Ted Sydney-based bon viveur. His recipes in *Oh for a French Wife* and those in Wallace Irwin's *The Garrulous Gourmet* appeared in the decade after World War II. They exerted a profound influence on that generation and lit the dawn of the current eminence of Australian cuisine.

Peterson, Heidi Oenologist, daughter of the super consultant Richard Peterson; both co-judge with the author at the Los Angeles County Fair.

Poilane, Lionel Master baker of Paris. His huge loaves of rye blend sourdough are flown fresh daily, available in Knightsbridge, London.

Power, Irma Master of East/West fusion cooking before the concept achieved its present usage. Wife of Justice Noel Power, president of the Hong Kong branch of the International Wine and Food Society, founder of the Pacific Rim Wine Exhibition.

Redman, Bill The man, and family, at the fountainhead of the first major phase of the development and recognition of the Coonawarra region premium red wines.

Ripe, Cherry Influential Australian food writer (including *Goodbye Culinary Cringe*), philosopher, creative chef.

Saunders, Charles Master palate, California-based. Co-judge, Los Angeles County Fair.

Skinner, Lou Generous oenophile, author, dermatologist, proud driver of a huge white Rolls Royce, of Coral Gables, Florida. Celebrates each decade with friends from around the world with a comprehensive tasting of '61 Bordeaux.

Stephanie Nom de cuisine of S. Alexander, top restaurateur of Hawthorn in Melbourne and influential food writer and philosopher. Leading candidate for culinary sainthood.

Sutcliffe, Serena MW London-based wine writer, director of Sotheby's wine section, wife of David Peppercorn MW, who was good enough to teach me the flavour of the Bordeaux grape, *Petit Verdot*.

Thomas, John Chef of the Year, 1986 and 1993, NSW Wine and Food Society.

Thomas, Richard Influential master Australian cheesemaker, one of the most innovative biologists I have met. He is the Thomas with a gold earring.

Watson, Jimmy His Carlton, Melbourne bistro was the first to select, and sell by the glass, great Australian wines. His in-group, 'The House of Lords', fostered some of the best palates in Melbourne, quite a statement considering their numbers generally.

Wright, Hilary Lecturer in Food Science, University of Western Sydney.

Acknowledgments

May I warmly thank the following friends and colleagues for their help. Jancis Robinson, Master of Wine, whose excellence as a wine writer, educator and television producer is exceeded only by the calls on her time, and thus the generosity of her Foreword. Michele Field, for her attempts to lead me in the paths of editorial righteousness. Brian McMahon, who is exactly the editor for me. Viv Thompson, for introducing me to the new thrust in matching wine and food in Japan. And Professor (Emeritus) Maynard Amerine, Tak Nishizawa, Dr Naoya Funaki, John Elliott, Hilary Wright, Professor Richard Hosking, Dr Julian Lee, as well as others mentioned in the text, and, not least, my wife Joy and family.

Recommended Reading

Athenaeus. Translated by Gulick. *The Deipnosophists*. London: William Heineman, 1967.

A gastronomic marathon, some fun. Two thousand years old and doesn't date.

Brillat-Savarin, Jean Anthelme. Translated by R.E. Anderson. *Gastronomy as a Fine Art*. London: Chatto and Windus, 1876.

Manners and mores of last century France. He made the most of what was available at that time.

Coultate, Tom. *Food, The Chemistry of Its Components*. 2d ed. London: Royal Society of Chemistry, 1989.

Ensrud, Barbara. *Wine with Food*. New York: Simon and Schuster, 1991.

A seasonal approach to the food, and a knockout section on pasta accompaniments.

Kanman, Madeleine. *In Madeleine's Kitchen*. New York: Collier, 1992.

Klivington, Kenneth, ed. *The Science of Mind*. Cambridge, Mass.: MIT Press, 1989.

Easy reading on mind, neurotransmitters, limbic system.

Lake, Max. 'The Marriage of Wine and Food.' *Epicurean*, August 1971, p. 30.

———. 'The Marriage of Wine and Food.' Wine Baron oration, University of Western Australia, 1992.

———. *Start to Taste* series, 1984–5.

Reitz, Carl. *A Guide to the Selection, Combination and Cooking of Foods*. Vol. 1. Connecticut: AVI Publishing, 1961.

A neglected and highly original, opinionated contribution.

Rosengarten, David, and Wesson, Joshua. *Red Wine with Fish*. New York: Simon and Schuster, 1989. Also bimonthly magazines.

Stimulating, thorough and a classic menu collection. *The* book for those who want recipes.

Steiman, Harvey. 'Wine and Food Made Simple.' A24 in 'The ultimate guide to buying wine.' *Wine Spectator*, 1993.

His regular contributions to *Wine Spectator* are a must for anyone with the slightest interest in the subject. The graphic depictions of wine sizes (*Wine Spectator*, p. 22, vol. XVI, no. 15, 15 Nov. 1991) are an easy guide for the perplexed.

———. 'Mixing Up the Menu.' *Wine Spectator*, 15 April 1994, p. 41.

A new paradigm for formal dining.

Watanabe, Masazumi, and Fujiwara, Masao. 'Compatibility of Wine and Cuisine.' Rep. 9th Internat. Oenological Symposium, Cascias, Portugal, 1990.

State of the Nipponese art.

Index

A

acetic acid 18, 34, 89
acid 63
   lift 35
acidity 50, 67
   adjusting 35
aftertaste 18, 33, 89
alcohol 50, 67, 68
aldehydic 83
Alexander, Stephanie 48, 56, 99
almond 43
Alsace 53
ambience 77, 79
   see also host
amino acids 37
Amoore, John 83
amphibians 20
amygdala 91
anchovies 40, 84, 95
androstenone 39, 40, 83, 84, 92
animal 83
   aromas 43
anise 43
apes 23
apocrine glands 92
apple 43
apricot 43
aromas 41, 42
   animal 43
   families 14, 21

arrack 38
arrowroot 70
artichokes 69
arugula 45, 84
asparagus 43, 84
Aspartame 86
astringency 17, 36, 68
Athenaeus 76
Australian Wine and Food Society 49

B

baby 16, 93
bacterial effects 64
balance 26, 31, 50, 53, 67, 78
   of sugar and acid 35
balsamic 83
barbecue ('barbie') 38, 67, 69
Barolo 69
Barossa Valley 56
basil 38
beans 37
beansprouts 83
beef 20, 43, 53
beer 27, 38, 87
Beer, Maggie 56, 96
Beeston, John 58, 96
beetroot 70
Beetroot marmalade (recipe) 71
bell pepper 22, 37, 94

Beppi's 68, 96
Beringer Vineyards 55
    Cabernet Sauvignon 71
berry
    black 43
    red 43
beurre blanc 70
Beychevelle 97
BHV centre 91
bitter 15, 16, 23, 34, 55, 64, 68, 86, 91
bitters 55
blachan 26, 39, 95
black currant 40
bloodhound 21
boarmeat 84
body 50, 53, 60
Bohdan, Tony 96
bone dry 86
Bordeaux 52, 53, 69, 99
Bordelaise 69
Borose, M de 80
bouquet 33, 39, 42
Bourbon whisky 43
brain 93
    scan 21
    stem 15
brandy 69
Brane-Cantenac 47
bread 45, 56
breathing 91
bridge 38
Brillat-Savarin 76
bubbles 53, 58, 72
Burgundy 43, 69
    red 70
    white 53
butter 43, 49, 53, 77, 83
Buttery, Ron 96

C

Cabernet 40, 43, 45, 51, 92
    oak-matured 40
Cabernet Franc 42
Cabernet Sauvignon 37, 39, 40, 42, 53, 63, 84, 85
Caillard, Andrew MW 97
camphor 83
capers 68
capsicum 22, 37, 94
caramel 37, 67
carbohydrates
    complex 48
cardinal principle of flavour and fragrance 26
carnation 38
carrot 34, 84
carta musica 56
cashew 43
cassis 40
caviar 69, 84
cedar 39, 40, 83
celery 84, 92
cells 20, 91
    regulation of 16, 19
    sexual activity 20
cerebral
    cortex 19, 91
    hemispheres 21
Chablis 45, 53, 89
champagne 39, 50, 63, 84
Chardonnay 42, 52, 53, 58, 84
Chateau d'Yquem 72
cheese 32, 39, 43, 44, 57, 77
    blue 58
    Brie 58
    cream cheese 58
    goat 58
    Gorgonzola 58, 69
    mozzarella 58

Munster 58
   sheep-milk 56
   soft 58, 84
   triple creams 58
cheesemaker 99
cheesy 83, 93
chef 23, 46, 75
   young 62, 72
chef/sommelier's brain 21
chemical contact sense 16, 18
cherry, Morella 61
chestnuts 84
Chevron Friday table 24, 96
Chianti 53
chicken 45
Child, Julia 25, 70
children 13
chilli 17, 26, 36, 64
China 49
Chinese
   restaurants 69
   roast duck 50
chocolate 38, 69, 95
cholesterol 49
Christie, Frank 96
chutneys 70
cider 27, 36, 50
cinnamon 38, 43, 83
citrus 43, 83
   zest 55
Clark, Courtney 54, 96
Clarke, Oz 36, 96
classic matches 51
cloves 38, 43, 83
cobber 92
cockie 92
cocoa 38
coffee 34, 38, 87, 95
cold 33, 41
composition of the sea 35

confit 70
contact 16, 18
contrast 50, 78
Coonawarra 98
coriander 84
Cornell University Hospitality
    School 55
cornstarch 70, 71
cortex 91, 94
   evolved from smell 19
   see also mind-body unity
Corti, Daryl 68, 96
Corvo 53
cost and quality 78
Costa Smeralda 56
coulis 70
cranial nerves 91
Crawford, Lydia 56, 96
cream 49, 53
crocodiles 20
cucumber 44
cuisines 12
curry 32, 36, 50
cyclamate 86

D

Damien, Manuel 72, 97
danger warnings 22
Dao 53
David, Elizabeth 70, 97
Davis, Ted 79, 97
deglazing 69
delight 26
demi-glace 47
dill 43, 52
dinner 67, 75
disgust 26
dominance of sight 91
Dr Jacobson's organ 20
dressings 70

dry 33, 86
duck 61
   Chinese roast 50
   stock 71
Duck-neck Sausage 48
Dupleix, Jill 44

E
earthworm 14, 16
earthy 43
East/West fusion cooking 62, 98
Elliott, John 100
embryo 93
emotion 39, 94
emotional drives 91
endorphins 23, 26, 27, 91, 92
energy marker 33
Entrecôte 69
essences 67
ethnic cuisines 58, 63, 70
   annihilation of Western wine flavours 26, 69
   see also chilli, curry
   see also Japan
Evans, Len 96
evolution 26, 31, 91
exotica erotica 44, 50

F
Falernian wine 49
Farwell, George 97
fast food 9
fat 36, 78
   component 64
   emulsions 41
   saturated 48, 49
fatigue 18
fatty 83
fennel 38
FIC 31, 32, 35, 36, 37, 38, 40, 52, 53, 61, 64, 67, 69, 72

Field, Michele 100
figs 44, 57
fire 37
fish 39, 64, 93
   casserole 50
   flaky 53
   oily 53
   poached schnapper 68
   sauces 26, 95
Fisher, MFK 70
fishy 83
five spices 71
flambé 67
flavour 13, 14, 20
   boosters 39, 69
   bridges 67
   cascade 16
   green 70
   impact 22
   impact compound (*see* FIC) 31
   markers 22
   matches 11 ff.
   power 51, 69
   see also regional
flintiness 89
floral 38
Florentine Renaissance 76
food
   colour 24
   colour test 24
   matching 41
   on aircraft 36
Food Options 79, 97
fragrance 20
free nerve endings 36
frog 93
fruit 43, 68
   flavour 33
   juices 35

fruity 38
fruity wines 36
Fumé Blanc 37
Funaki, Naoya 100
fusion cooking 62, 98

G

Gamay 42
game birds 53
garlic 64
gastronomy 49, 75, 80
German wines 63
Gibson, Victor 49, 97
ginger 71
glass 17
glucose 86
glutamate 32, 93
glutamine 93
golden ages of the smell brain 19
gooseberries 37
grana padana 57
Grant, Yvonne 45, 97
grapefruit 43
grapes 34
   see variety
grass 43
Gray, Patience 75
green 37, 83
   Chartreuse 43
   flavour 70, 94
grill 67
growing season 24
Guide Michelin 23
gutsier tucker 93

H

ham 44, 47, 68
happy hormones 26, 91, 92
hardness 89
hazel 43
head food 25, 69
heart 91
hedgehog 20
hedonic rating 93
herbs 38, 43
Hermitage 42
hippocampus 91
Hiroshima Champagne Society 97
Hom, Ken 46, 62, 97
home cooking 10, 75
honey 39, 56, 68, 92
hormones 39, 94
Hosking, Richard 97, 100
host, keystone of the meal 59
hot food 41
hot/cold 17
housewives 75
human embryo evolutionary replay 20
Hungarian goulash 37
hunger 91
hydrochloric acid 34
hypothalamus 19, 91, 93

I

Ikeda, Kikunae 15
IMP 22, 37, 94
incense 79
inhibition 21
insects 38
International Wine and Food Society 78, 98
Irwin, Wallace 70, 98
isomers 93
Italian red 50
IVA 39, 84, 93
Ivan's Aperitif 25

J

Jackson, Cynthia 72, 97, 98
Jackson, Ted 72
Jacobson, organ of 20, 93
Japan 58, 61, 63, 69, 79
jasmine 33
Johnson, Hugh 97
Joseph, Robert 36, 98

K

Kanman, Madeleine 55
keystone 59
kidney 44
kim chee 64
Kiwi fruit 37, 42, 43
koala 20, 21, 23
Kodo 79

L

label drinking 24
lactic acid 34, 64
lactose 86
lamb 53
Lang, Barbara 55
leather 43
Lee, Julian 100
lemon 33, 35, 43, 55, 83
lemon myrtle 56
less is more 40, 95
Levy, Paul 25, 98
Levy, Penny 25
light 37
limbic system 19, 91
lime 33, 43
    juice 34, 87
Limousin oak 42, 85
liquorice 38
Little Snail 72
Livornese 68
Los Angeles County Fair 98

Lucas Carton 46
lychees 50

M

mace 83
madeira 38, 39, 47, 84
    truffled 43
Maillard, Dr 37, 67
Malbec 42
malic acid 18, 34, 89
maple syrup 68
Marchand de Vin 69
marinades 67
markets, food and fish 72
marmalade 70
    beetroot 71
masking 33, 41, 63, 68, 93
Mason, Jacqui 57, 98
Mason, Warren 57, 98
master sauces 48, 70
    recipe 71
mawkish 89
McGee, Harold 78, 85
McMahon, Brian 100
meal
    centre point of 46
meat 64
medicinal 83
Mediterranean 26
medulla 91
Melbourne 99
melon 50
    green 43
Memmel oak 42
memory 91
Merlot 42
metallic 17, 32, 83
micro-organisms 58
middle palate 34
milk 35, 87

milky 83
mind-body unity 19, 91, 94
mineral 83
mint 38, 43, 56
minty 83
MIP 22, 37, 94
Missouri oak 42
Mocha coffee 34
Moloney, Ted 70, 98
Mondavi, Robert 11
monkeys 35
Morella cherry 61
Mosel 53
mossy 83
mother 23
mother sauces 70
mouth 91
mouth-feel 17, 33
Mouton-Rothschild 52
MSG 16, 23, 31, 93, 95
Muscadet 53
Muscat 38, 42, 58
mushrooms 32
music
   soft 78
musk 39, 40, 83, 92
musky 83
mustard 17, 26, 36, 69
mutton 53
myrtle 56

N

nectarine 43, 56
neurotransmitter 39, 92, 94
Nevers oak 42
Nishizawa, Tak 100
NSW Wine and Food Society 79, 97, 99
nutmeg 44
Nutrasweet 86

nutritional essentials 22
nuts 43
   roasted 38

O

oak 11, 83, 85, 92
   barrels 38
   flavour 38
   forests 42
   see also Limousin oak
odour
   blindness 5, 20, 21, 92
   components of an 21
   discrimination 21
   drive, as a threat 21
   sensors 91
oil 35, 36, 44, 70
olfaction 39, 91
   primacy 23
olfactory nerves 91
olive oil 57, 70
olives, green 37
onion 34, 68, 71
orange 25, 43, 83
   juice 70
ouzo 38
oxalic acid 34
oxidation 9
oxidisation 38
Oyster Bar 54
oysters 39, 45, 54, 84

P

Pacific Rim cuisine 3
Pacific Rim Wine Exhibition 98
pain 27
pain/pungent 17
Pak Poy, Timothy 40
palate 5, 27, 61
   length 17, 18, 34, 89
   preference 35, 58

Parma ham 57
parmesan 32, 45
Parmigiano 57
parsley 45, 84
pasta 50
pastes 40
pâté 50
peach 43, 50
pear 43, 45
Peking dried mushrooms 71
pepper 26, 38, 43, 83
Peppercorn, David MW 99
perfumer 23
pernod 38, 43
persimmon 84
Peterson, Heidi 98
Peterson, Richard 98
Petit Verdot 42, 99
pH 87
pheromones 15, 20, 39, 85, 94, 95
   human sexual 83
   pheromonal FICs 39
   trail 38
pigeon 71
Pinot 18, 51, 53, 84
Pinot Blanc 53
Pinot Grigio 53
Pinot Gris 53
Pinot Noir 42, 53, 58
pituitary pouch taste analogue 93
placenta 92
planning dishes around a special wine 62
Poilane, Lionel 98
pork 20, 53, 56
port 69
Portugese wine (Dao) 53
postcentral gyrus 17, 94
potatoes 35
poultry 53
powdery 83
Power, Irma 71, 98
Power, Noel 98
prawn 40, 84
   rotting 95
preference 20
pressurised cabins 36
primacy 23
primary tastes 17
professional 75
prosciutto 50, 56
pungent 26, 36
purées 70
pyrazine 37, 94
pyrroline 83, 84

Q

quaffing wine 57
Queen's bee 94
quince 43

R

Rabelais, François 22
reaction, Maillard 37
readiness to perceive 2, 13
redcurrant 47
Redman, Bill 98
reductions 40, 48
refrigeration 9
Regency College (Adelaide) 55
regional
   food 69, 75
   matches 55, 56
reptiles 20, 23, 93
resinous 83
Reyniére, Grimod de la 76
rhubarb 34
rice 35, 39
richness 53
Riedel Glass 17

Riesling 42, 53, 84
Ripe, Cherry 99
roast beef 38, 39
roasts 38
Robinson, Jancis xii, 100
rocket 45, 84
Rome 49, 79
rosé 50, 53
rosemary 56
Rosengarten, David 54
rosewater 38

S

saccharin 86
sake 63, 64
salad 45, 64
salmon 51
  smoked 50
salsas 70
salt 16, 26, 35
  tracks and roads 35
  water 45
salty 15, 91
  foods 68
sandalwood 39, 40
Sardinia 56
Sardo 56
saturated fat 48, 49
sauces 40, 67, 84
  reduced wine sauce 69
  sauce base 55
  mother 70
sauerkraut 44
Saunders, Charles 70, 99
sausage 44, 47, 48, 52
Sauternes 45, 50, 86
Sauvignon Blanc 37, 42, 58, 70, 71
sea water 35
seafood 54

seasonal variation in fat content 64
seasonal foods 4
secondary fermentation 34
Semillon 42, 70
sensory mix 79
sequence 13, 59, 77
  wine 76
sex 19
sexual
  function 39
  invitations 22
  pheromones 78
  pheromones, human 83
  smell brain function in humans 20
sexuality 91
shelf life 4, 10
shellfish 53
Shinto kitchen god 61
Shiraz 42, 53
Simon, André 49, 77
sirloin 64, 69
sizes 33, 48, 51, 52, 53, 58
skatole 83
Skinner, Lou 99
smell 17, 21, 95
  messages 95
smell brain 17, 19, 91, 95
  accessory sexual 20
Soave 53
social table v
Society of Wine Educators 54
sodium 35
solitary nucleus 15, 91, 95
sommelier 21, 23, 46, 59, 68
sotolon 32
soubise 34
soul 62
sour 15, 16, 34, 35, 91

sourdough 35, 98
South-East Asian cuisine 26, 34, 38, 39
soya sauce 71
Spanish wine 53, 68
sparkling wine 53
spermous 83
spices 38, 43
spicy 38, 83
spinach 37, 44
spirit of the chef 62
spiritual association with wine and food 62
stale socks 92
star anise 71
starches 35
steak 44
Steiman, Harvey 54, 55
Stephanie, *see* Alexander, Stephanie
stews 67
sticky 50, 69, 86
stock 26, 32, 48, 55, 67, 70, 71
stroganoff 52
sugar 35, 37, 86
   excessive 26
   reducing 33
   residual 33
sun 37
super smeller 23
Sutcliffe, Serena MW 99
sweat 43
sweaty 83, 84
sweet 15, 16, 33, 91
sweet hay 43
sweetness 34, 63, 68, 78
   in wine 68
Sydney International Wine Competition 57, 98
Sydney Seafood School 54
symposium 49, 76
synergism 32, 68, 95, 96
synesthesia 79
synthetic 32

T

table 78
tangerine 25
tannin 18, 36, 41, 50, 55, 63, 89
tartaric acid 18, 34, 89
taste 14, 17, 18, 21, 91, 93
taste brain 15, 91
   worm's 17
tasting glass 17
tea 33, 38
temperature 41, 60, 77
temporal lobe 91
Tetsuya Wakuda 46, 62
texture/crunch 17
thalamus 17, 91, 95
thiamin (vitamin B1) 22
Thomas, John 70, 99
Thomas, Richard 58, 99
Thompson, Viv 100
threshold 40, 95
throat 91
thyme 56, 70
TMA 39, 40, 95
toasts 38
toasty-roasty 95
tofu 70
Tokyo 63
tomato 68, 87
   concentrates 32
tongue 15, 47, 91
training 21, 23, 92
Traminer 27, 38, 42, 53
trigeminal 17, 95
truffle 39, 40, 43, 47, 84, 85

U

umami 15, 16, 23, 32, 91, 93
unity
    mind/body 19
urine 92

V

Valpolicella 53
vanilla 43, 83, 84, 85
vas deferens 92
veal 53
    stock 70
    stroganoff 52
vegetable 83
vegetable aromas 43
vegetables 64
    pickled 64
venison 53, 64
Verdelho 58
vermouth 25, 34, 43
Victoria 56
vinaigrette 68, 70
vinegar 34, 35, 44, 70, 87
    aroma 89
vitamin C 22
vomeronasal organ 20
vomeronasal system in human embryo 93
vomiting 91
vomitorium 49

W

wasabe 36
water 87
Watson, Jimmy 99
wedding breakfast at Cana 59
weight 72
    see also size
Wesson, Joshua 54
whisky 38, 69
wild cards 68

Willan, Anne 55
wine 44, 55, 87
    acidic 68
    acids 18
    aging 89
    aromas 42
    astringent 68
    bouquet 42
    cooking 67
    dry 60
    flat flavoured 68
    Italian 50, 53
    judging 23, 57
    pop 'pearl' 50
    red, aged 89
    sequences 59, 60
    Spanish 68
    sparkling 53
    spoilage 89
    styles 48
    temperature 41, 63
    young 60
    see also Bordeaux, Burgundy, Coonawarra, Portugese wine, sequence
Wine and Food Society of Australia 97
    see also NSW Wine and Food Society 97
wine or food cultures 57
Wine Spectator 54
wine taster's brain 21
winemaker 23, 35
woody 83
    see also oak
worms 23, 85, 91
Wright, Hilary 63, 99, 100

Y

yeast 42, 43
yoghurt 27, 44, 70

A loaf of bread,
a jug of wine,
and thou ... are enough.